Pictures for Writing

By David A. Sohn

HART DAY LEAVITT, EDITORIAL CONSULTANT

BANTAM BOOKS

BANTAM PATHFINDER EDITIONS
NEW YORK / TORONTO / LONDON

RLI: $\dfrac{\text{VLM 7.0}}{\text{IL 6.12}}$

PICTURES FOR WRITING
A Bantam Pathfinder edition / published October 1969

*All rights reserved.
Copyright © 1969 by Bantam Books, Inc.
This book may not be reproduced in whole or in part, by mimeograph or any other means, without permission.
For information address: Bantam Books, Inc.*

Published simultaneously in the United States and Canada

Bantam Books are published by Bantam Books, Inc., a National General company. Its trade-mark, consisting of the words "Bantam Books" and the portrayal of a bantam, is registered in the United States Patent Office and in other countries. Marca Registrada. Bantam Books, Inc., 666 Fifth Avenue, New York, N.Y. 10019.

PRINTED IN THE UNITED STATES OF AMERICA

ACKNOWLEDGMENT—PICTURES FOR WRITING

Excerpt from **Cheri** by Colette Copyright 1951 by Farrar, Straus & Young, and reprinted by permission of Farrar, Straus and Giroux.

Excerpt from **A Separate Peace** by John Knowles © 1959 by John Knowles, and reprinted by permission of The Macmillan Company.

Excerpt from **The Sound and the Fury** by William Faulkner Copyright 1929 and renewed 1957 by William Faulkner; Copyright 1946 by Random House, Inc., reprinted with their permission and that of Curtis Brown, Ltd.

Excerpt from **Out of Africa** by Isak Dinesen Copyright 1937 and renewed 1965 by Rungestedlund-Jorden; reprinted by permission of Random House, Inc. and The Bodley Head, Ltd.

Excerpt from "North Fayer Hall" in **The Anatomy Lesson and Other Stories** by Evan S. Connell, Jr., Copyright 1953 by Evan S. Connell, Jr.; reprinted by permission of The Viking Press, Inc.

Excerpt from "A Texas Suburb of the Moon," by Dorothy Jane Hamblin, in **Life**, December 16, 1968, © 1968 by Time, Inc., and reprinted with their permission.

Excerpt from "Rain" by W. Somerset Maugham in **The Trembling of a Leaf** Copyright 1921 by Smart Set & Co., reprinted by permission of Doubleday & Co., Inc. and A. P. Watt & Co.

Excerpt from "A Little Cloud" by James Joyce in **Dubliners** © 1967 by The Estate of James Joyce. Reprinted by permission of The Viking Press, Inc. and Jonathan Cape, Ltd.

Excerpt from "Bliss" by Katherine Mansfield Copyright 1920 by Alfred A. Knopf, Inc. and renewed 1948 by John Middleton Murry. Reprinted from **The Short Stories of Katherine Mansfield** by permission of Random House, Inc. and The Society of Authors.

Excerpt from **Winesburg, Ohio** by Sherwood Anderson Copyright 1919 by B. W. Huebsch & Co.; renewed 1947 by Eleanor Copenhave Anderson. Reprinted by permission of The Viking Press, Inc. and Jonathan Cape, Ltd.

Excerpt from "A Curtain of Green" by Eudora Welty in **A Curtain of Green and Other Stories** Copyright 1938, 1966 by Eudora Welty. Reprinted by permission of Harcourt, Brace & World, Inc.

Contents

Introduction	6
Looking At The World	10
Using Your Senses	20
Setting The Scene And Mood	43
Articles, Narratives, Letters, Reports	62
People	82
Point Of View	104
Conversation	122
Plot: Dramatic Tension	139
Surprise And Comedy	155
Fantasy And Symbolism	174
Acknowledgments	190

Introduction

Why do you write? To communicate, to send a message to someone. Putting words on paper is a better, faster way of sending messages than smoke signals, drumming across the jungle treetops, or tapping out Morse code. Written messages can travel farther (through time and through space) and can reach more people.

The essence of good writing is choosing the words that carry your message most clearly. If your writing is not good enough—if you pick a wrong or unsuitable word, or string words together sloppily—your message may not get through at all, or will be misunderstood. Here is an example of a garbled message, an advertisement from a Japanese maker of electric toothbrushes:

Everybody speak about a wonder of Dental Shinning in Europe and U.S.A.

Here we present "PEARL DENTAL SHINNER" which protects a delicate children's gum and make the good and shiny teeth automatically.

What is Dental Shinning?

It is a special method to clean the teeth shiny by giving the teeth smooth vibration and massage with Battery Operated Tooth Brush.

Of course, it requires the new improved Dental Cream at the same time.

As a result of a long painstaking study of making the good teeth, a modern scintists find a way to give an effect from the surface of teeth or gum to inner tissue, then the dental creem with Fluorine or Vitamine B see the light.

However this new Dental Cream with Fluorine can not do her job alone without "DENTAL SHINNER." The physical motion of PEARL DENTAL SHINNER eliminate the scum and dirty of foods, namely 600 cycle second of vibration and massage settle the problem reasonably.

Now you understand what the "DENTAL SHINNING" is!

If you had never heard of an electric toothbrush, would that confused account make you rush out to buy one? No? Then the message didn't get through.

Even when English is your own familiar language, you have to be careful that what you write is what you mean, and that you choose words and phrases that are clear, descriptive and right. Written messages cannot, like spoken words, be helped by facial expressions, hand gestures or explanations of what you really mean. The written words have to speak clearly for themselves. Otherwise, just as if you had dropped the drumstick or tapped the wrong telegraph key, your message will not get through.

If you leave out an important detail, your friend won't know which corner of Elm Street you want to meet him on at three o'clock. If your account of your abilities and past work is muddled, you won't get the job you want. If the instructions you have written are not precise enough, the engineer may hurt himself or damage the equipment he is trying to assemble from your technical manual. If the emotions in your love letter come tumbling out onto the page in too much of a jumble, your girl may miss your real message—that you'd like to marry her. And if your Broadway play is boring, the audience will doze off by the second act.

Everyone can learn to write better. A few people, with talent and much hard work, learn to write so well that they become professionals, communicating to thousands of readers. Their magazine articles, plays, poems and novels—even their diaries and personal letters—may be read and reread by people all over the world, through centuries. What is their secret?

The great writers of the past and present differ completely from one another in the style of their language, in the literary forms they use, and in the way they see the world. But hidden in that last phrase you just read is their common "secret." They all do *see* the world. They notice everything. They observe the shapes and colors of nature, the sounds of city streets, the smells of a country kitchen. They watch the tiny movements of people's eyes and fingers, and listen to the way people talk when they feel angry or afraid. Nothing is too small or too big to escape their attention. Like the best police detectives of fiction, they develop their skill of observation until it becomes second nature. When they enter a room, their keen senses unconsciously register every detail and emotion in it.

Professional writers watch the whole of life. They think about what it may mean, and life's meaning is the complex and individual "message" they send to their readers ... telling them about the humor and subtlety of mankind, the richness of living, the beauty and variety of the surrounding world.

Their world and their lives are completely different from those of the many, many people who drift through their waking hours, half asleep, pleasantly numb. Life is not really *lived* by those who automatically follow their daily routine like robots, without seeing much, hearing much, feeling much or understanding much of what goes on around them. It is all too easy to gulp down lunch without tasting it, while flipping the pages of a magazine without really reading it; to travel to school or work every morning, without noticing anything new or unusual along the way; to chew candy absent-mindedly, without enjoying it; and to have the radio or television on, without actually watching or listening.

"The paradoxical situation with a vast number of people today is that they are half asleep when awake, and half awake when asleep, or when they want to be asleep," psychoanalyst Erich Fromm has written. "To be fully awake is the condition for not being bored, or being boring." Being awake is necessary for experiencing a full, interesting life. It is certainly the first step toward becoming a good writer.

Wake up, then! Even if you think you're more interested in

getting fun out of life than in learning to write, practice using all your senses, one by one. How much do you really *see* what you look at? What color eyes does your brother or best friend have? What was your mother wearing this morning? What lies outside the window you stare through every day?

Look at a person for about ten seconds. Then turn your head away. Try to describe his clothes, shoes, hair and eyes. Shut your eyes for a few minutes now. Listen to how many different sounds you can hear, near and far, including some so familiar (like a clock ticking) that you usually shut them out.

This book gives you a plan for practicing writing and improving your skill at it. It is based on the idea that to write well, you have to be observant, and then interpret what you have seen with accuracy and imagination. By showing you how much there is to see in a picture, this book will help you become more observant and more skillful at writing about what you see.

If you work at it steadily, day by day, you will soon find yourself seeing more in the world around you, and thinking more about what you have seen. You will face a sheet of blank paper with confidence, and find that writing is fun, because you will have gradually strengthened your imagination and your ease with words.

You can never expect to write well if you do not practice by writing something, even a diary, every day. It is as challenging to turn words into writing as it is to make notes into music. It takes just as much practice.

Another point to remember is that no piece of writing will be as good as it could be if you write it only once. Good writers revise and polish their efforts many times. They cut out unnecessary words, replace passable phrases with better ones, until they have created their very best. Months, often years, of very hard work go into the greatest books and plays. Like the smooth, strong performance of a professional athlete, this kind of polished writing looks easy only to those who have never tried it themselves.

10

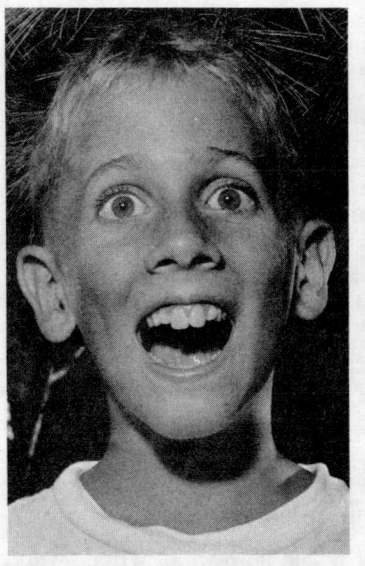
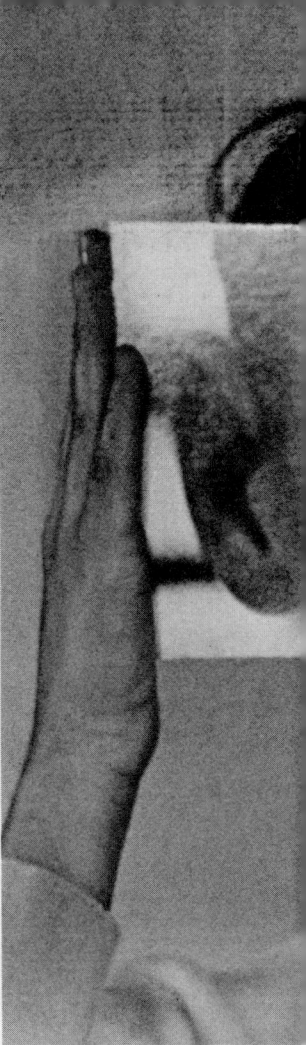

Looking At The World

There is a new world out there every day, every hour, every minute.

Observe! There is surprise for the eyes, ears, nose, tongue, fingers, all the senses. There is great joy in discovery.

14

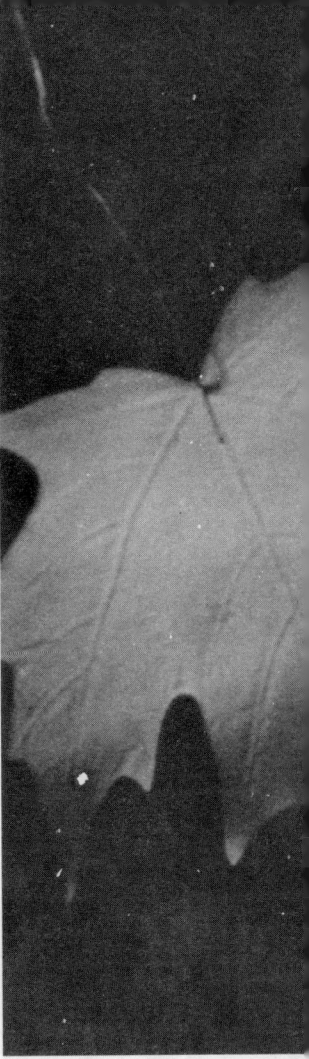

Birds and squirrels must look out to stay alive.

16

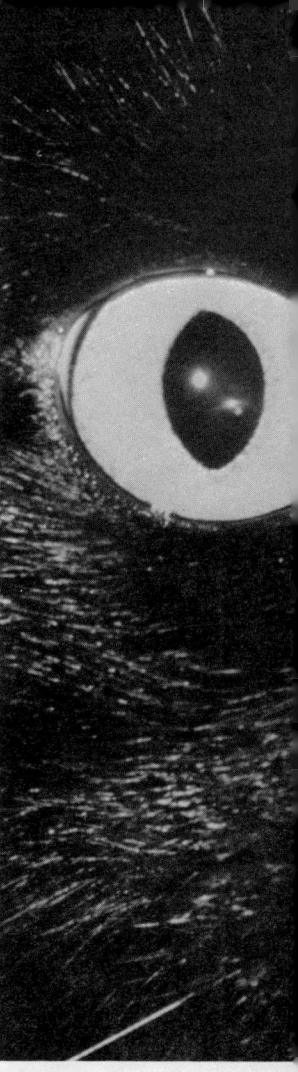

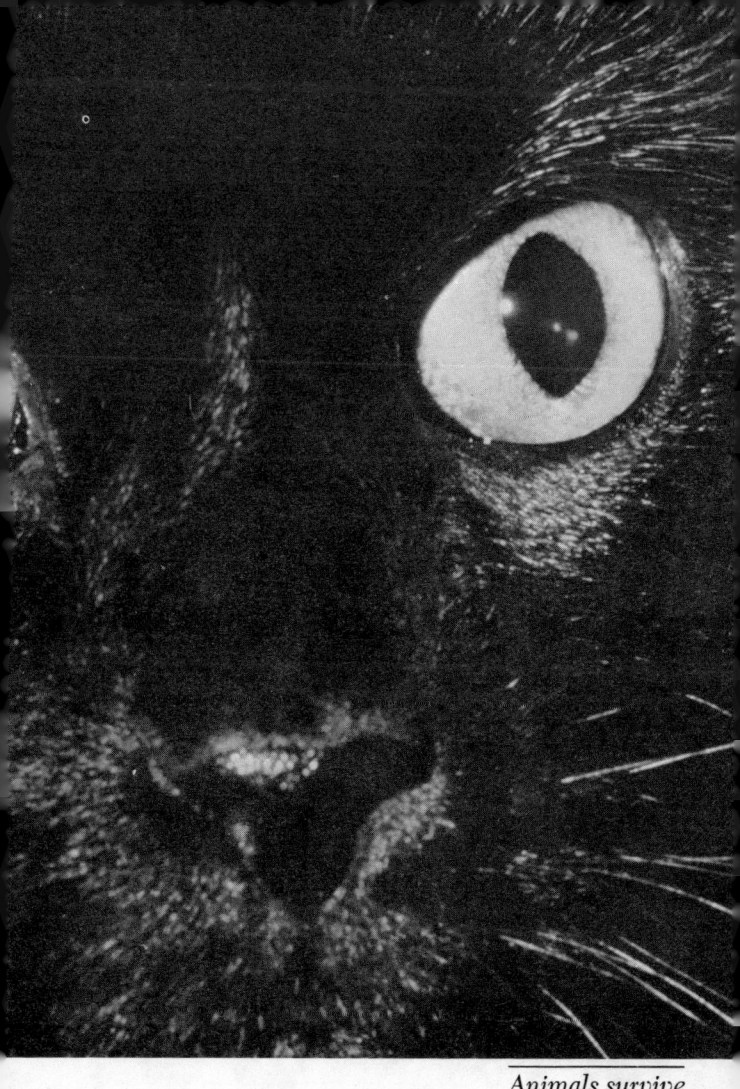

Animals survive through all their senses. So does man.

The hunter sees more than the trees and the forest. The writer sees more than other people. Use all your senses. Stop, look, and listen. Feel, taste, and smell. Then write.

Using Your Senses

You do not see things only with your eyes. When you really look at an object, with awareness and concentration, you unconsciously add information from your other senses to what your eyes tell you.

Exercise 1:

Look at an object, now. Use your eyes to see its color, size and shape. Then reach out to feel it, or use your imagination to guess what texture and warmth it would have if you touched it. Is it rough? Silky? Cool? Hard? Grainy? Polished? What sounds might it make if you banged or tapped it? Does it have any scent or taste?

We tend to let our eyes do all the work. Growing babies are not like us. They have to put all objects into their mouths to discover their feel, size, shape and taste, because they have not yet learned to get this information through their eyes. Blind people, too, see with their other senses. They can lead people who can see through thick fog or a power failure, because they have learned to hear echoes, the sound of water, traffic and machinery; they feel the hill slope under their feet, or the pavement change; they smell the daytime scents from the coffee shop or shoe factory, and know which way the wind is blowing them.

Exercise 2:

Imagine that you are looking at a galloping horse. Listen to the thud of its hooves, and to all background noises from the track or stables. Breathe in the smell of the horses themselves, and of the crushed grass or sun-warmed earth. Imagine how the horse feels the strength of its muscles, the rush of the wind, and the ground's texture.

Always look at everything around you—and at the pictures in this book—with all five senses and, most important of all, with your sense of imagination. A writer uses sensory words so that we can see and feel and smell and taste and hear along with him, as if we were there.

For example, instead of just telling us that Léa paused for a few moments in the garden, the French writer Colette makes us actually live those minutes with the heroine of her novel:

Léa stopped for a moment by the door, then stepped out into the garden. She picked a tea-

rose, which shed its petals. She listened to the breeze in the birch, to the trams in the Avenue, to the whistle of the local train. The bench she sat on was warm, and she closed her eyes, letting her shoulders enjoy the warmth of the sun.
—Colette, *Chéri*

Exercise 3:

Notice how specific Colette is, telling us that the flower was a tea-rose, that the tree was a birch, and that it was the local train that whistled. Make a careful list of absolutely everything Léa saw, smelled, heard and felt.

Next time you read a good story, count how many times the author appeals to your five senses when he creates a scene. Read Tennyson's poem "The Lotos-Eaters," if you can find a copy, and notice all the lush sights, rich colors, sounds, feelings, exotic smells and tastes experienced by the exhausted sailors who beached on the tropical island.

If you let your senses work for you, you can learn to make places and events come alive for your readers, too.

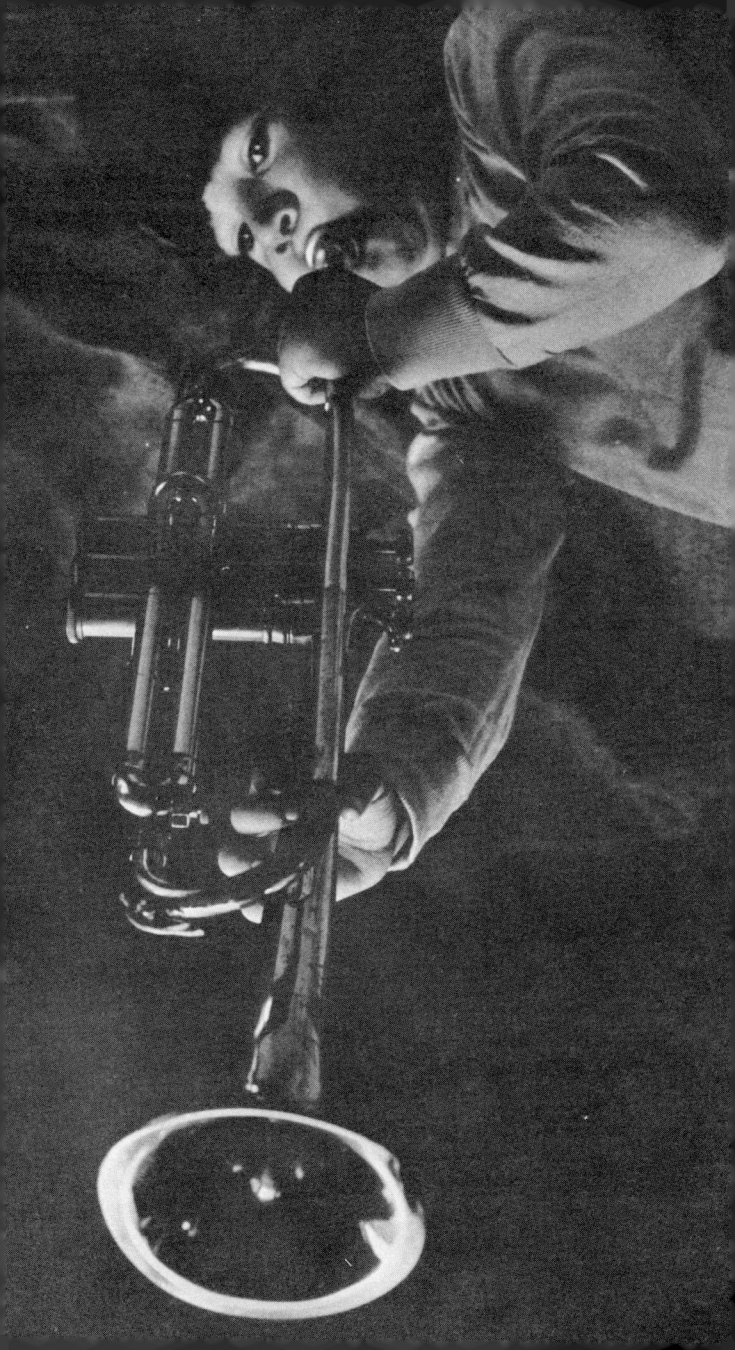

Sound
Exercise 4:

Here is an exercise in sound. Imagine that you are standing near the child on this page. Describe his struggles with his horn, by writing a list of all possible noises that might come out of it as he tries to play it. What you write does not always have to be whole words. Just try to create the sounds you might hear. Make up as many as you can.

Many real words are vivid descriptions of sounds. Have you ever heard the whippoorwill, a bird named for its call? Many everyday words represent the sounds they mean: *clang, buzz, grate, roar, tinkle*.

Exercise 5:

How many other "sound" words can you write down? Can you find *tintinnabulation* in your dictionary?!

Writers and poets are often clever at choosing words with sounds that suggest what they are describing. Stress the "mmm" and "zzz" sounds, as you say aloud:

> The moan of doves in immemorial elms,
> And murmuring of innumerable bees.

Exercise 6:

Make up a few phrases reproducing the noise of wind, bells, heavy traffic, or any sound you like. You do not have to write complete sentences.

Listen to the vivid way John Knowles describes the sounds at a private school:

> Phineas stopped talking for once, so that now I could hear cricket noises and bird cries of dusk, a gymnasium truck gunning along an empty athletic road a quarter of a mile away, a burst of faint, isolated laughter carried to us from the back door of the gym, and then over all, cool

> and matriarchal, the six o'clock bell from the Academy Building cupola, the calmest, most carrying bell toll in the world, civilized, calm, invincible, and final. —John Knowles, *A Separate Peace*

These are the early-morning sounds in a Mississippi kitchen, around 1930:

> After awhile it ceased to flap. Dilsey prepared to make biscuit. As she ground the sifter steadily above the bread board, she sang, to herself at first, something without particular tune or words, repetitive, mournful and plaintive, austere, as she ground a faint, steady snowing of flour onto the breadboard. The stove had begun to heat the room and to fill it with murmurous minors of the fire, and presently she was singing louder, as if her voice too had been thawed out by the growing warmth, and then Mrs Compson called her name again from within the house. Dilsey raised her face as if her eyes could and did penetrate the walls and ceiling and saw the old woman in her quilted dressing gown at the head of the stairs, calling her name with machine-like regularity. —William Faulkner, *The Sound and the Fury*

Sight

Look at this picture of animals, pretending that you have never seen them before and do not even know that rhinoceroses exist. You are an explorer in Africa, the first Westerner ever to see them. What do these amazing creatures really look like to fresh eyes?

Exercise 7:

Write several sentences about the picture, describing the animals to people back home, who have never seen them. What are their shapes and colors? How do they move? How do they fit in with the landscape? Most important, what do they remind you of?

Resemblances and comparisons are the heart of interesting writing. This is true whether you are describing objects, people or moods. A writer may say one thing is *like* another, using a figure of speech called a *simile*. "I wandered lonely as a *cloud*," wrote Wordsworth, describing his detachment from the world and people.

A writer may go further, using a *metaphor* to say that one thing actually *is* another, possessing its qualities. "The Lord is my *shepherd*" (Psalm 23). "My mind to me a *kingdom* is" (Sir Edward Dyer). "All the world's a *stage*, / And all the men and women merely *players*" (Shakespeare).

We all speak in similes and metaphors every day. We say that the wind howls (like a wolf), and that an idea dawns (like the day). We say we boil with anger, or freeze with fear. We often choose phrases like this because we have heard them so often—Bill ate like a horse, Mary is a dream, John is strong as an ox, Joe is dull as dishwater.

Exercise 8:

Complete these phrases with the obvious, common word:

Straight as an . . . . . .
Quiet as a . . . . . .
Warm as . . . . . .
Pretty as a . . . . . .
Black as . . . . . .
Light as a . . . . . .
Busy as a . . . . . .

There were no "right" answers in the exercise above. The point is, you filled in the words without having to think for yourself. The phrases were *clichés*, expressions worn out through too much use. Because we have all heard those comparisons so many times, they no longer bring a picture to our minds. Clichés are tempting because they are so easy. But they are dull. Avoid them!

Compare the clichés above with these comparisons used by poets and novelists. Which are better?

"As straight as a beggar can spit..." (Kipling)

"Quiet as despair..." (Robert Browning)

"Warm as a sunned cat..." (Thomas Hardy)

"As hot as peppered brandy..." (William King)

"Cold as a dead man's nose..." (Shakespeare)

"Blacker than a raven in a coal mine..." (O. Henry)

"Dark as a sullen cloud before the sun..." (Byron)

"Light as flake of foam..." (Hans Christian Andersen)

"Busy as a cow's tail in fly time..." (J. Fenimore Cooper)

Stretch your imagination (and your reader's) and use your power of observation to invent comparisons that surprise, shock and please because they are so new and true.

Isak Dinesen was a Danish baroness who ran a coffee plantation in Kenya, East Africa, some forty years ago. Notice the similes and metaphors she chose to describe the animals she saw. Notice all the shapes:

> I had time after time watched the progression across the plain of the Giraffe, in their queer inimitable, vegetative gracefulness, as if it were not a herd of animals but a family of rare, long-stemmed, speckled gigantic flowers slowly advancing. I had followed two Rhinos on their morning promenade, when they were sniffing and snorting in the air of the dawn,—which is so cold that it hurts in the nose,—and looked like two very big angular stones rollicking in the long valley and enjoying life together.
> —Isak Dinesen, *Out of Africa*

Exercise 9:

Can you write three or four sentences to describe an American pet or farm animal as if you had never seen it before?

Touch

What does it really feel like to wash your hands?

Exercise 10:

Use your memory and imagination as you look at this picture. Write three or four sentences, describing the feel of hot and cold water, soap and bubbles, your wet hands rubbing one another, the dry towel. (If you like, add a few extra sentences for your other senses, describing how the process sounds, what the bubbles look like, how the soap smells and tastes). Try to make up some good comparisons.

Taste And Smell

The cook in this picture earns his living by using his trained tongue and nose, as well as his eyes and fingers.

Exercise 11:

Write a few sentences about the possible taste and smell of the foods the cook is preparing for a party. Are they sour? Sweet? Spicy? Bland? Sticky? How do they feel on the tongue? A little girl once said that soda pop tasted like her foot was asleep.

Exercise 11a:

Can you describe the most exotic or unusual food you have ever eaten? What do toasted marshmallows taste like? Why do you like your favorite food and drink?

No locker room could have more pungent air than Devon's; sweat predominated, but it was richly mingled with smells of paraffin and singed rubber, of soaked wool and liniment, and for those who could interpret it, of exhaustion, lost hope and triumph and bodies battling against each other. I thought it anything but a bad smell. It was preeminently the smell of the human body after it had been used to the limit, such a smell as has meaning and poignance for any athlete...
—John Knowles, *A Separate Peace*

OKRA

Nauseating green vegetable.
Fried in butter, you are unbearable.
Stringy, yet slimy,
Boiled you are worse.
Of a consistency like
Greasy bubblegum,
You seem to expand as I chew you.
Is this your death agony?
Or are you merely
Warning me in a friendly way,
Not to swallow you?
—Eighth grade student

The Five Senses

Use all your senses (sight, sound, touch, taste and smell), as you study the next three pictures.

Exercise 12:

List the following details, giving a sentence or two to each.

1. What is the man wearing?
2. What is the boy wearing?
3. What is the man sitting on?
4. What is the boy sitting on?
5. Are all the birds alike? How do they differ, if they do?
6. What very small details can you see?
7. What sounds does the boy hear?
8. What does the boy smell or taste?
9. What does the boy feel with his body?
10. Describe the man's expression. What kind of attitude does his posture suggest?
11. How do you think the boy feels? Why?
12. What do you think the man is saying to the boy?

Exercise 13:

Notice all the details you can about the little girl and her kitten. Then choose one of the two following situations, and write a paragraph about the picture. Write at least ten sentences.

1. The little girl is blind. Pretend you are the girl, telling someone else what you can feel about your pet. Use all your senses except sight.
2. Pretend you are the kitten, learning about new sights and sounds every day as you grow bigger. The girl looks huge to you. How does her voice sound? What do her hands and bare chest feel like? Does she smell of shampoo, or taste of soap, perhaps? Are you afraid?

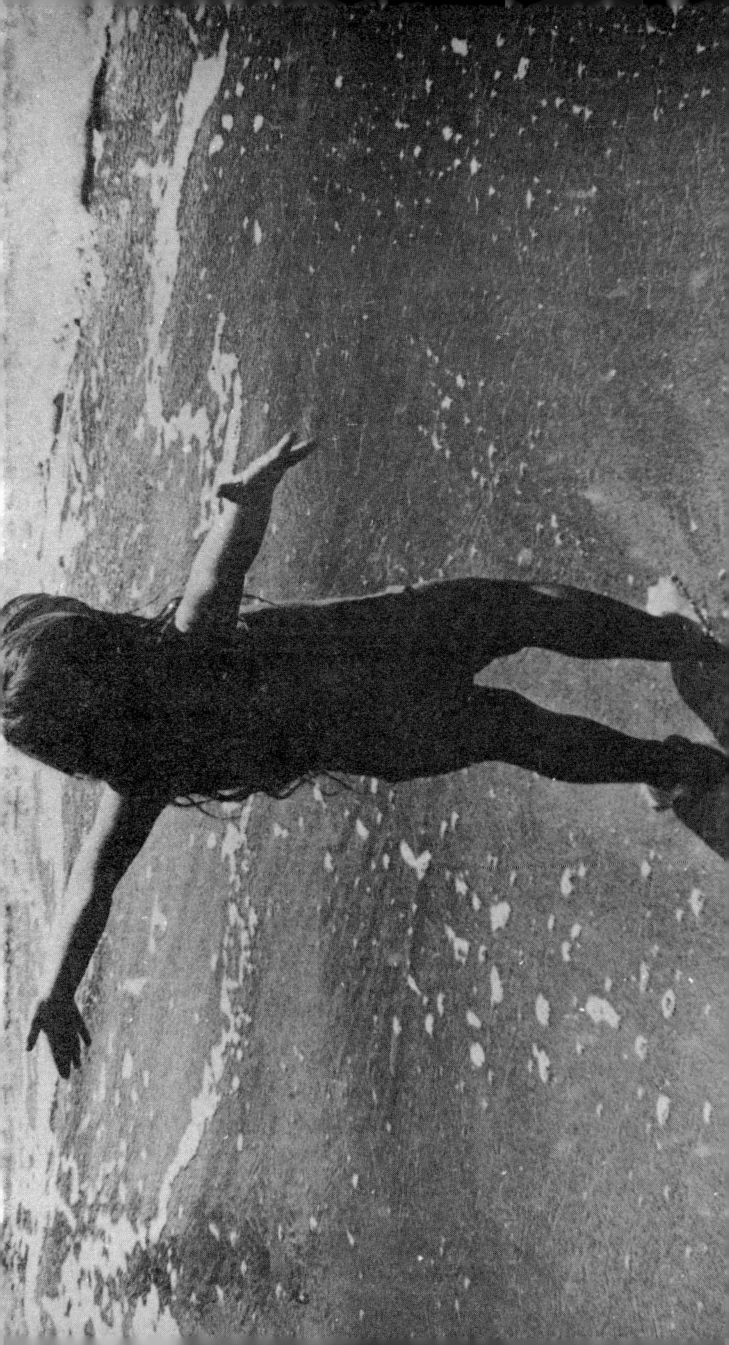

Exercise 14:

The little girl on the beach on this page is obviously enjoying herself. Put yourself in her place, and imagine her sensations. Then complete the sentences below, making up good comparisons to describe the sensations.

1. The sand and water under her toes feel like . . .
2. The sun warms her body like . . .
3. The white surf looks like . . .
4. The spray on her lips tastes like . . .
5. The waves sound like . . .

Finally, write a paragraph of several sentences, joining together the comparisons you have made above. Use them as the basis for a description of the girl's feelings and her happiness. Write in the first person ("I"), if you like.

Exercise 15:

How many senses are referred to in this writing by a ninth-grade student? What other sense descriptions can you imagine to add to this description of dissecting worms?

> The girls in the lunch line were discussing the earthworm dissection which they had just completed the period before in biology . . .
>
> "It really wasn't so bad, except that they were all floating around in a jar of junk that looked like . . . well, anyway, they were all dried up and gutsy looking," Pam said.
>
> "Oh, I thought they were delicious. I mean beautiful. That is, except for the smell," Sue admitted.
>
> "What did it smell like?" Joan asked.
>
> Sue frowned slightly and thought for a moment. Then, shrugging her shoulders, she replied, "I dunno. Dried up worm guts, I guess."

The girl standing behind Penny opened her eyes a little wider and seemed to turn a shade whiter. The others went on.

"Did you see that strange kid who sits next to me?"

"No, who?" Joan interrupted.

"Oh, you know, the one who is short, fat with buck teeth. He looks like a hungry gopher."

"Oh yeah, I know," Joan said.

"Well, anyway, he stuck a scalpel in the middle of the worm and got a squirt of blood all over his face."

The girl's face flinched as a wave of green passed over it. Even so, she couldn't bring herself to turn away. She kept listening.. "Oh, I had a real flatworm. He was probably a criminal or something. His whole intestine was completely filled with dirt."

"Mine was all white and sickly, and he looked sorta like a big fink. Probably spent all his time turning over soil in some little old lady's garden." Pam chortled.

The others laughed and asked Meg, who had kept quiet, what she thought of the dissection.

"I thought it was kind of disgusting. They felt all slimy like wet rubber or plastic," Meg shuddered.

The silent girl standing behind Penny looked up toward the ceiling, then muttered, "Oh, gross," and walked away from the line, suddenly deciding that she didn't want any lunch.

Setting The Scene And Mood

Place

A sense of place is crucial to most stories and novels, and to many other kinds of creative writing. A piece of fiction often begins by describing the scene where the action will happen. Like the setting of a stage play, this description of background lets the reader visualize where (and when) the actors are going to appear.

To create a setting that seems "real," a writer chooses significant details to describe. The more he singles out particular objects, colors, street names and sounds, the more vividly the reader can imagine that place.

Exercise 16:

Make a list of the colors, textures, sounds and smells in the art department's building described here:

> North Fayer Hall stood on the final and lowest hill of the university, a little askew from the other buildings as if it were ashamed of its shabbiness and had turned partly away. Its windowsills were pocked by cigarette burns and the doors of its green tin lockers had been pried open for so many years that few of them would lock any more; the creaking floors were streaked and spattered with drops of paint, dust lay upon the skylights, and because the ventilating system could not carry off so many fumes it seemed forever drenched in turpentine. Mercifully the little building was hidden each afternoon by the shadows of its huge, ivy-jacketed companions.
> —Evan S. Connell, Jr., "North Fayer Hall"

Exercise 17:

Using all your senses, write a few sentences about either of the next two pictures. Begin with the overall impressions of the whole scene. Then narrow your focus to specific details. Pick out shapes, colors, shadows, textures, feelings, sounds and smells. Make the place "real."

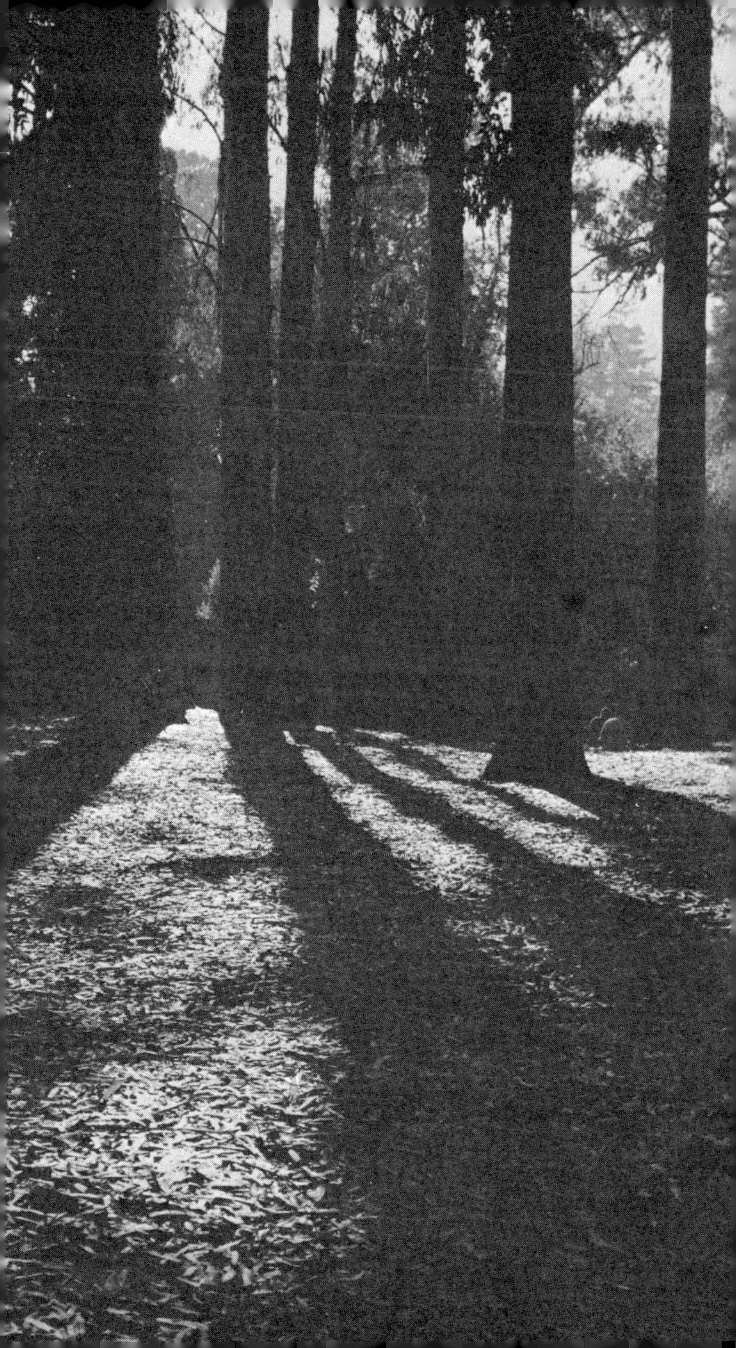

**WEBER'S
AUTO·SERVICE
EXPERT·REPAIRS**

47

The picture on the next two pages shows Japanese Shinto priests in the courtyard of the Meiji shrine in Tokyo. The photograph on page 50 is of an empty school corridor leading to the music department.

Exercise 18:

Choose one of these two places. Write half a page or more about it. Use your imagination, and invent sensations like the temperature, smells, possible colors and far-away sounds... Can you hear a student who has stayed late to practice, or the tinkle of temple bells?

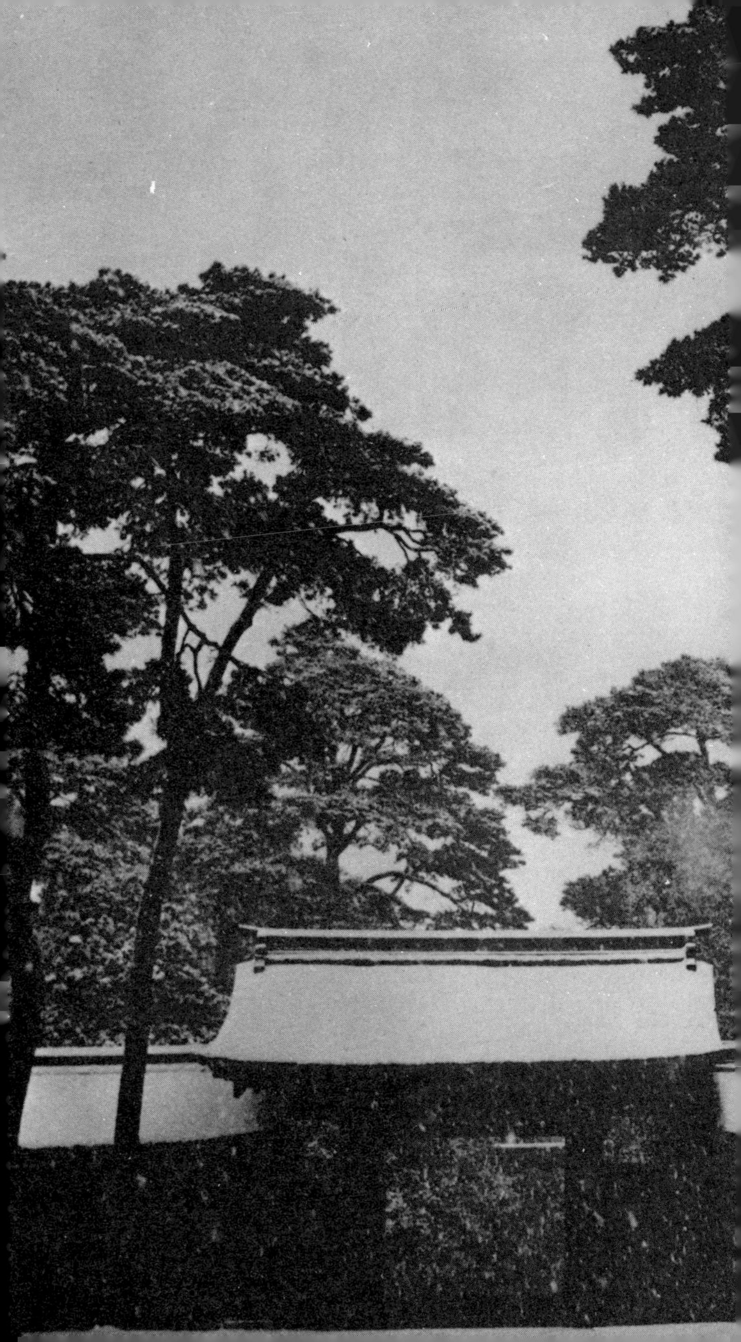

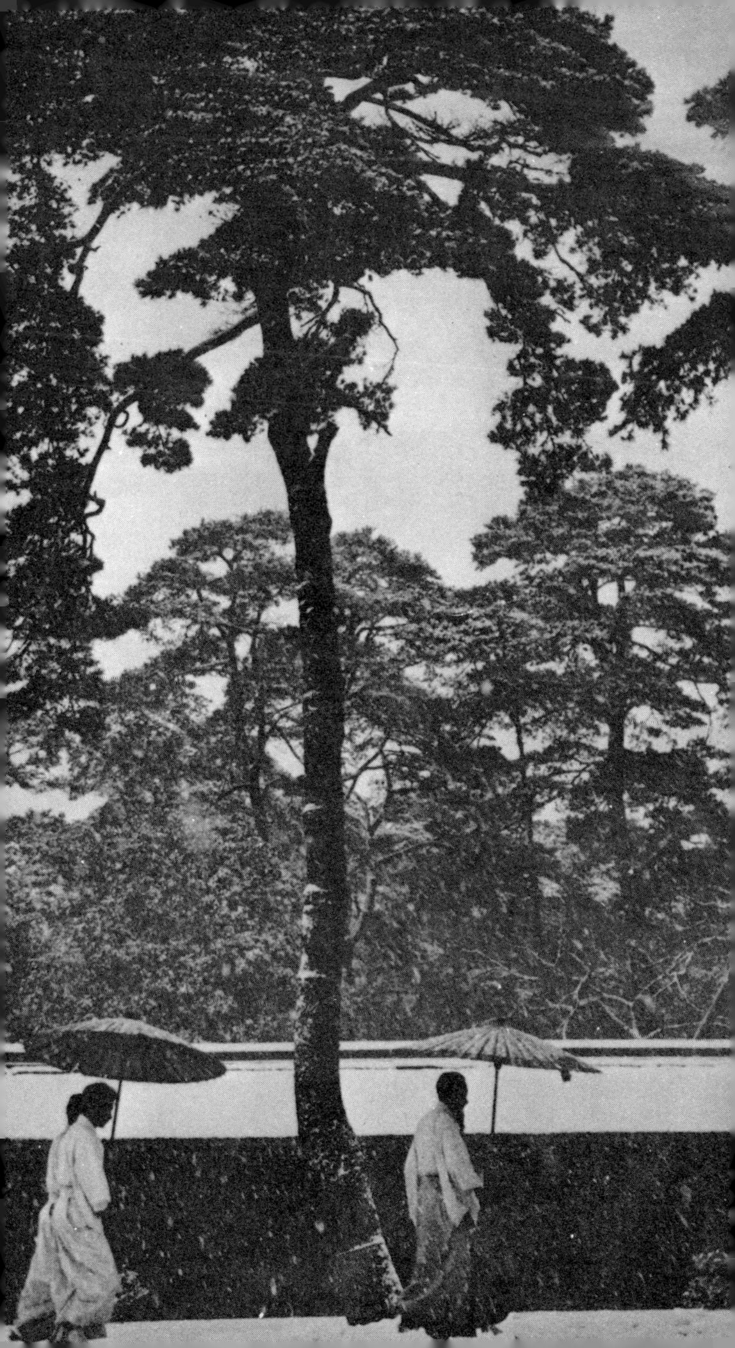

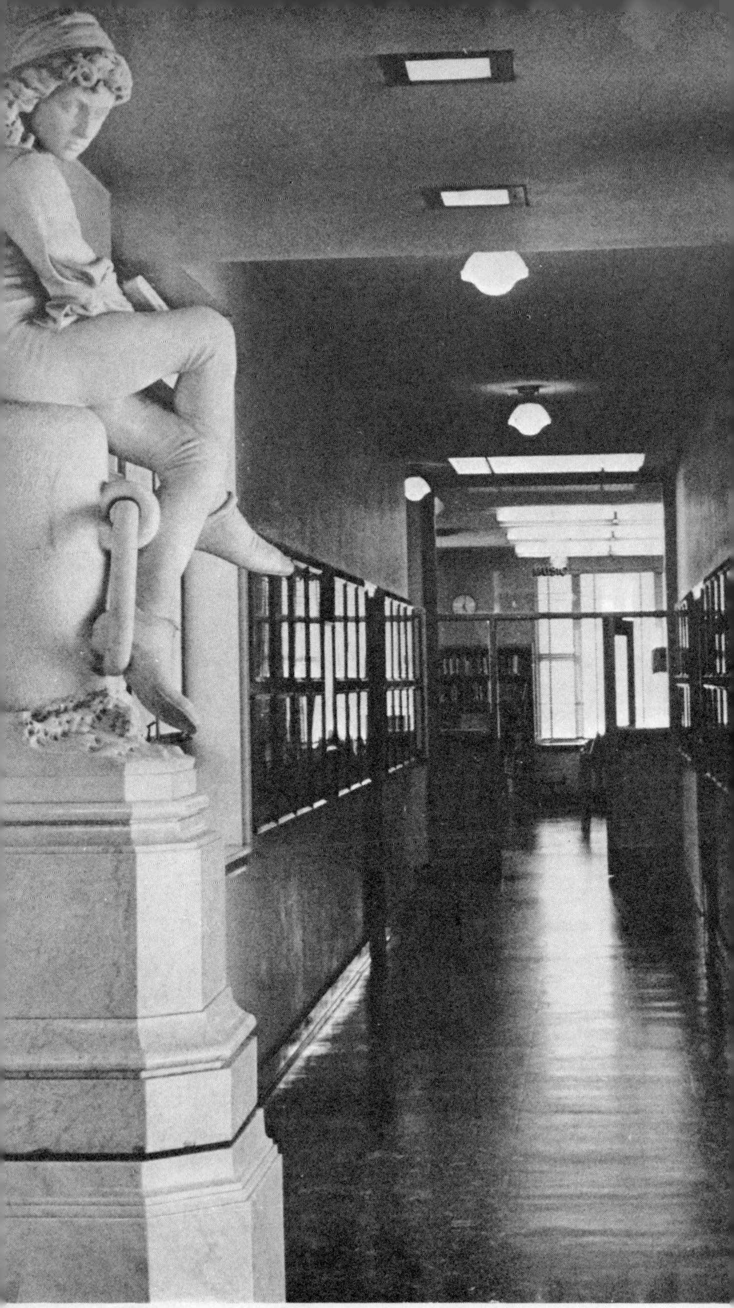

Details and comparisons make an imaginary place come alive for the reader. This realism is as important in journalism, which describes real places, as it is in fiction. Notice how journalist Dora Jane Hamblin uses revealing details to build up a vivid impression of the land near Houston where the Manned Spacecraft Center is located.

This is a land so flat that telephone poles take on a certain exotic charm; a land in which a coarse crabgrasslike greenery called St. Augustine's grass is cultivated tenderly because it's about the only grass which will grow (you have to sprinkle it regularly with sand, even so, or else the ground will get so hard the irrigating water just runs off). It is a land abounding in poisonous snakes, which have a disturbing habit of hatching inside the garden walls; in which street lights burn natural gas and are left to burn day and night because that's cheaper than setting up a force to turn them off; and in which the atmosphere is so hot and humid that to get a car without air conditioning you have to place a special order.

Where six years ago there was nothing but some cows, the center's director, Dr. Robert R. Gilruth, now looks out his office window at a community so new it looks like a movie set.
—Dora Jane Hamblin, "A Texas Suburb of the Moon"

Exercise 19:

What scenes and significant facts would you choose, if you wanted to tell a stranger about your home town? Write a page or two, describing it.

Mood

Descriptions of places can do much more than serve as backgrounds for a story's action. Often, in fiction, they set the *mood* or emotional tone for the whole story. They tell the reader, indirectly, whether the tale is going to be one of happiness or horror, mystery or love.

The setting matches the mood or atmosphere of the story. For example, you probably would not begin a sad story about a lonely old invalid by describing a sunny flower-filled garden...unless you deliberately wanted to shock your reader by the contrast.

When Matthew Arnold wrote a poem of mourning for his dead father, he set the scene—and mood—by describing the school where his father used to be the principal:

> Coldly, sadly descends
> The autumn-evening. The field
> Strewn with its dank yellow drifts
> Of wither'd leaves, and the elms,
> Fade into dimness apace,
> Silent;—hardly a shout
> From a few boys late at their play!
> The lights come out in the street,
> In the school-room windows;—
> —Matthew Arnold, "Rugby Chapel"

Why didn't Arnold describe the school in spring or summer? Why didn't he choose the scene at noon? Because those descriptions would have been inconsistent with the sad mood of his poem. They would have put the reader in the wrong frame of mind for what was to follow.

As soon as you read the beginning of Edgar Allan

Poe's story, "The Fall of the House of Usher," written over 100 years ago, you realize that a tale of horror and mystery is to follow:

During the whole of a dull, dark, and soundless day in the autumn of the year, when the clouds hung oppressively in the heavens, I had been passing alone, on horseback, through a singularly dreary tract of country; and at length found myself, as the shades of the evening drew on, within view of the melancholy House of Usher. I know not how it was—but, with the first glimpse of the building, a sense of insufferable gloom pervaded my spirit.

... I looked upon the scene before me—upon the mere house, and the simple landscape features of the domain, upon the bleak walls, upon the vacant eye-like windows, upon a few rank sedges, and upon a few white trunks of decayed trees—with an utter depression of soul....
—Edgar Allan Poe, "The Fall of the House of Usher"

Historical time can be an important part of the sense of place, if a story is set in the past. London as Charles Dickens knew it is obviously not the London of today. Instead of observing his own surroundings, an author who wants to write a historical story must read a lot about that other time and place. When it is familiar to him, he can recreate it for his readers.

Robert Louis Stevenson's story "The Sire de Malétroit's Door" is set in France during the English invasion of the Hundred Years War. In the year Stevenson mentions (below), Joan of Arc freed the city of Orleans and saw a French king crowned at Rheims. It was an exciting time.

Exercise 20:

Notice the historical details Stevenson uses to set the scene—the year, the men-at-arms, the English flag, the archways. Make a list of the phrases and words that put you in the *mood* for exciting adventure.

It was September, 1429; the weather had fallen sharp; a flighty piping wind, laden with showers, beat about the township; and the dead leaves ran riot along the streets. Here and there a window was already lighted up; and the noise of men-at-arms making merry over supper within, came forth in fits and was swallowed up and carried away by the wind. The night fell swiftly; the flag of England, fluttering on the spire top, grew ever fainter and fainter against the flying clouds—a black speck like a swallow in the tumultuous, leaden chaos of the sky. As the night fell the wind rose, and began to hoot under archways and roar amid the tree-tops in the valley below the town.

Denis de Beaulieu walked fast. . . .
—Robert Louis Stevenson, "The Sire de Malétroit's Door"

Exercise 21:

A door or a window often suggests mystery. What lies at the top of these stairs? How long has the place been deserted? Who may be about to enter? Study the picture. Then write five or six sentences about the place, referring to specific details and establishing a mood. The place may look frightening and mysterious to you, or sunny and friendly.

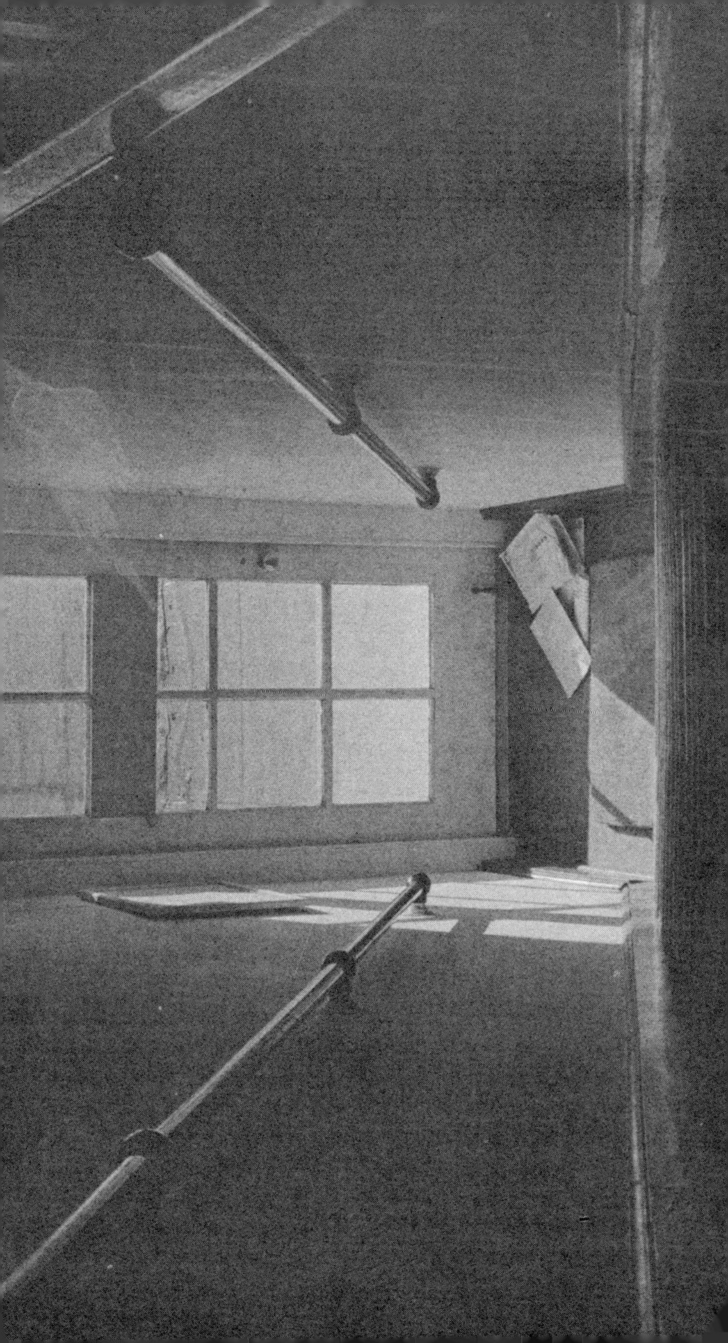

Exercise 22:

Choose this picture instead, if you prefer. Look at the discarded objects in the attic, and at the way the sun falls on them. Write ten sentences or more, describing the attic, and creating a mood as the beginning of a possible story about the girl. You don't have to write the whole story, just its start. But you may want to think ahead and answer these questions in your mind: is the girl lonely or happy? Is she thinking of the past or the future? Why is she alone in the attic?

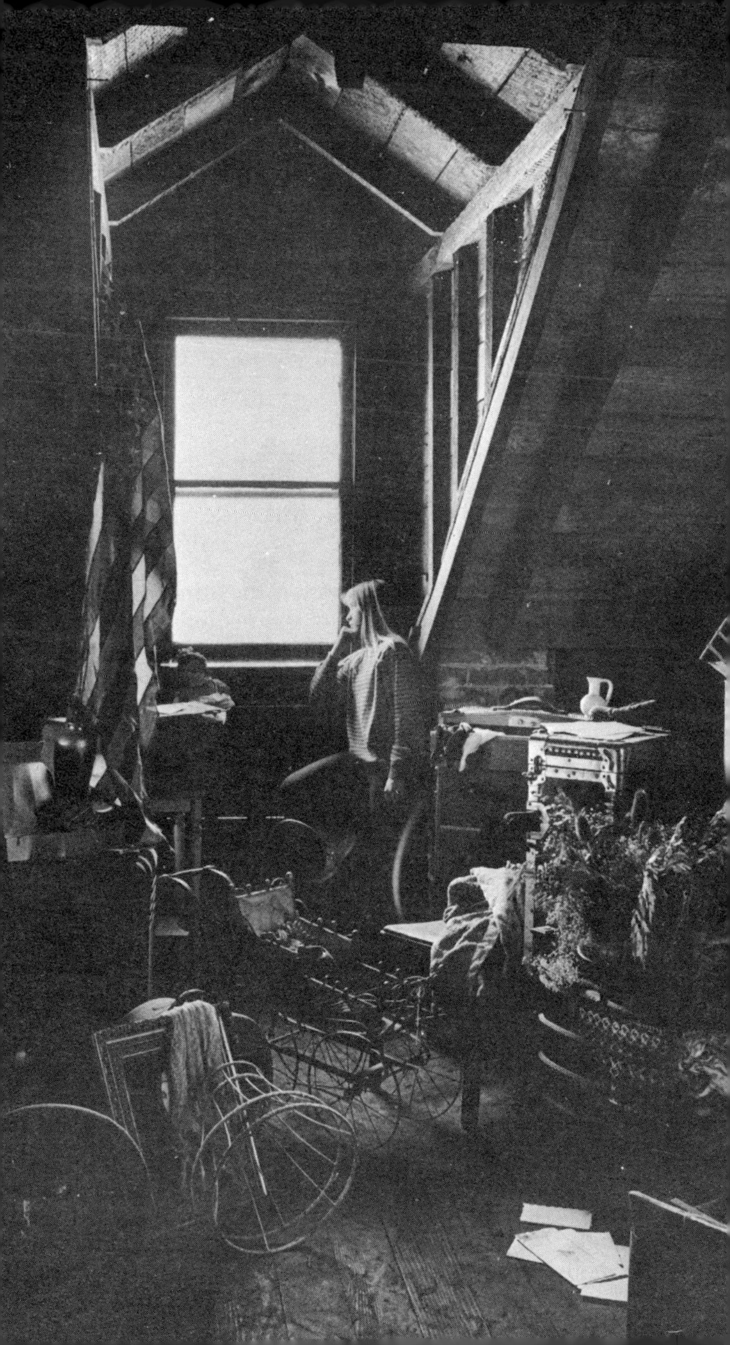

In the pictures and examples so far, the atmosphere of a place has been shown to affect the reader's emotions (and those of the character in the story). The opposite is also true. That is, the emotional state or mood of a person will affect the way a place looks to him. A terrified person will see dark shadows and terrors behind every bush. A happy, self-confident person will see beauty and good humor in unexpected places.

In James Joyce's story, "A Little Cloud", the hero is disillusioned with life and tired of his city, Dublin. He envies his old friend, who has made good in London. This is how he sees his own surroundings:

> He turned often from his tiresome writing to gaze out of the office window. The glow of a late autumn sunset covered the grass plots and walks. It cast a shower of kindly golden dust on the untidy nurses and decrepit old men who drowsed on the benches; it flickered upon all the moving figures—on the children who ran screaming along the gravel paths and on everyone who passed through the gardens. He watched the scene and thought of life; and (as always happened when he thought of life) he became sad.

... He emerged from under the feudal arch of the King's Inns, a neat modest figure, and walked swiftly down Henrietta Street. The golden sunset was waning and the air had grown sharp. A horde of grimy children populated the street. They stood or ran in the roadway or crawled up the steps before the gaping doors or squatted like mice upon the thresholds. Little Chandler gave them no thought. He picked his way deftly through all that minute vermin-like life and under the shadow of the gaunt spectral-like mansions in which the old nobility of Dublin had roystered.

—James Joyce, "A Little Cloud"

Exercise 23:

Look at the following picture of the beach. Choose whether to make the person in it sad or happy. Then write a page describing the scene through the person's eyes, establishing a definite mood. Explain whether the sun is setting or rising. Give a reason for the person's mood, and explain why he or she is walking alone at that hour. Use as many sensory details as you can, to make the place real, and to make the mood convincing.

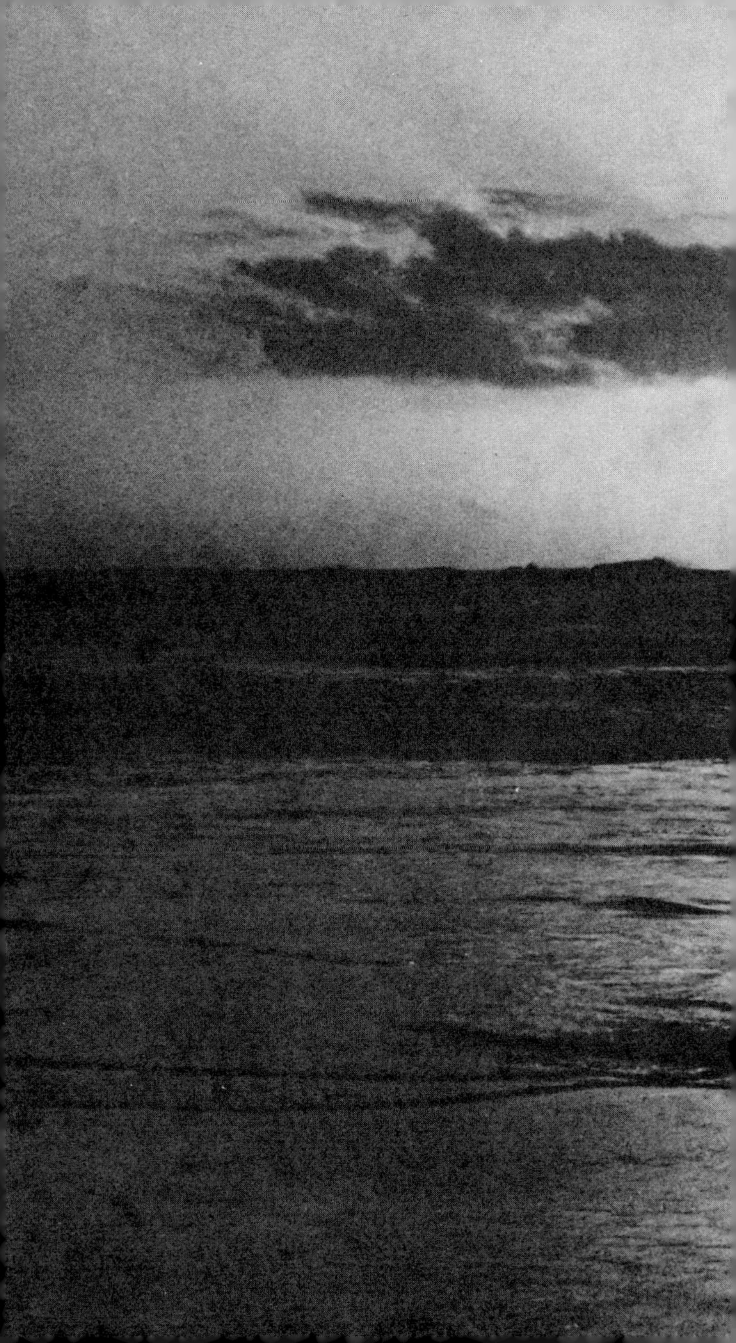

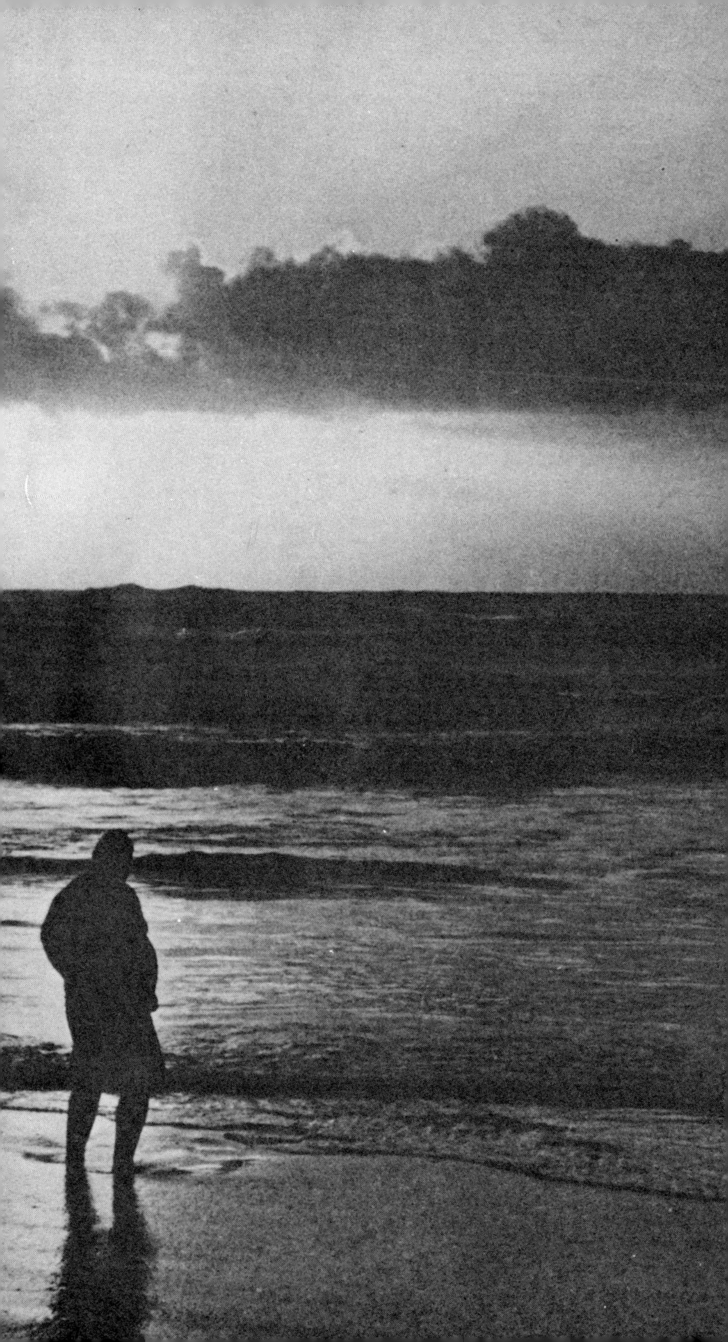

Articles, Narratives, Letters, Reports

Not many people become professional authors of short stories, novels or plays. But few of us spend a day without writing a letter, a diary, directions or instructions, or perhaps a report of some sort. Fiction is not the only form of writing that needs care, practice and imagination. In the kinds of writing most of us do every day, looking at details, inventing original comparisons, arranging thoughts in logical order, and influencing the reader's mood are vital techniques.

It is amazing, for example, how few people can give a stranger clear directions to a place. Either they have never opened their eyes to notice what lies along the route, or they can't arrange the signs and turns in proper order.

Exercise 24:

Write directions for a visitor, telling him how to drive or walk to your home from the nearest bus station (or railroad or airport). Do more than tell him when to turn left or right. Give him a vivid description of the buildings, scenes, sights and sounds he will pass on his way. Before you write this, you might want to travel the route yourself, jotting down notes as you go.

Exercise 25:

If you prefer, write instructions on how to make or build something. Write for someone who has never done anything like it before. For example, you might instruct your reader on the basic technique of a sport, such as skating, or the method of baking a fruit cake. Keep your instructions in a clear step-by-step order. But write more than a simple "recipe." Use many sensory details, to give your reader an idea of the actual experience.

Look carefully at the picture of the surfer on page 66. Notice all the physical details, and imagine what the sport feels like to his senses of sight, sound, touch, taste and smell.

Exercise 26:

Write a short "magazine article" (two pages) for readers of your own age, telling them about your experience of going surfing for the first time in your life. Make them feel the excitement and exhilaration, so that they will want to try it, too. Give your article an introduction and a conclusion—a beginning and end, as well as a middle. You may want to pretend you are writing this for a magazine you read, like *Boys' Life* or *Seventeen*. Use strong, active verbs to make your writing lively.

Here is how one student wrote about surfing. See if you can include even more details in your article.

> The great mass of greyish-blue water gushed forward into a new wave. Two figures out on the dark horizon were ready and waiting. The huge mountain of water billowed over, crashing into the water beneath it, and the white foam thundered along at a swift pace to meet the sandy shore. Both of the figures had tried to catch the wave, but the great tumbling mass surrounded and strangled one of them, then discarded him as it rolled along on its way with the other surfer on its back.

The clouds in the background drummed out their threats to those two surfers who dared remain out on the ocean into the late afternoon when the rain always came. The darkened sky seemed to have come swiftly, and they would have to get in quickly if they hoped to escape the merciless pellets of rain on their bare backs and the sharp lightning that always sliced its way through the air.

The one that had stayed on the wave was now gliding in the direction of the welcome sight of the shore as his surfboard skimmed the surface of the little ripples that danced around him. Then he washed onto the sand with a sudden explosion of terrific speed. He could feel the rocks and shells grind into the bottom of his newly painted board, then he scrunched to a stop.

When he recovered from the jolt, he turned and stared out onto what had been an angry sea. Now it was peaceful and still, and the remains of the sunlight that was not yet masked by the dark clouds made wavering reflections in the water. The air was warm to his sun-baked skin, but he could sense the rising humidity that forewarned the arrival of the afternoon thunderstorm. He gestured wildly in order to be seen by his companion who floated quietly in the water for another burst of power to carry him back to safety.

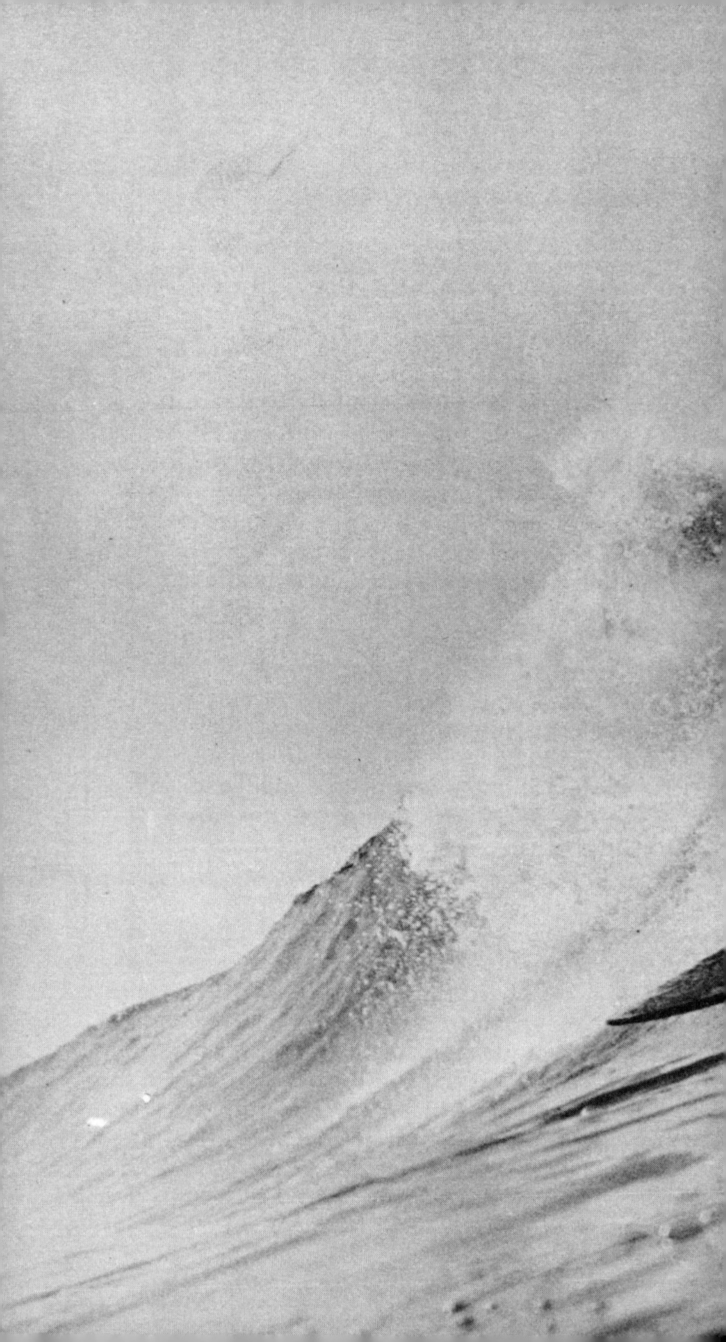

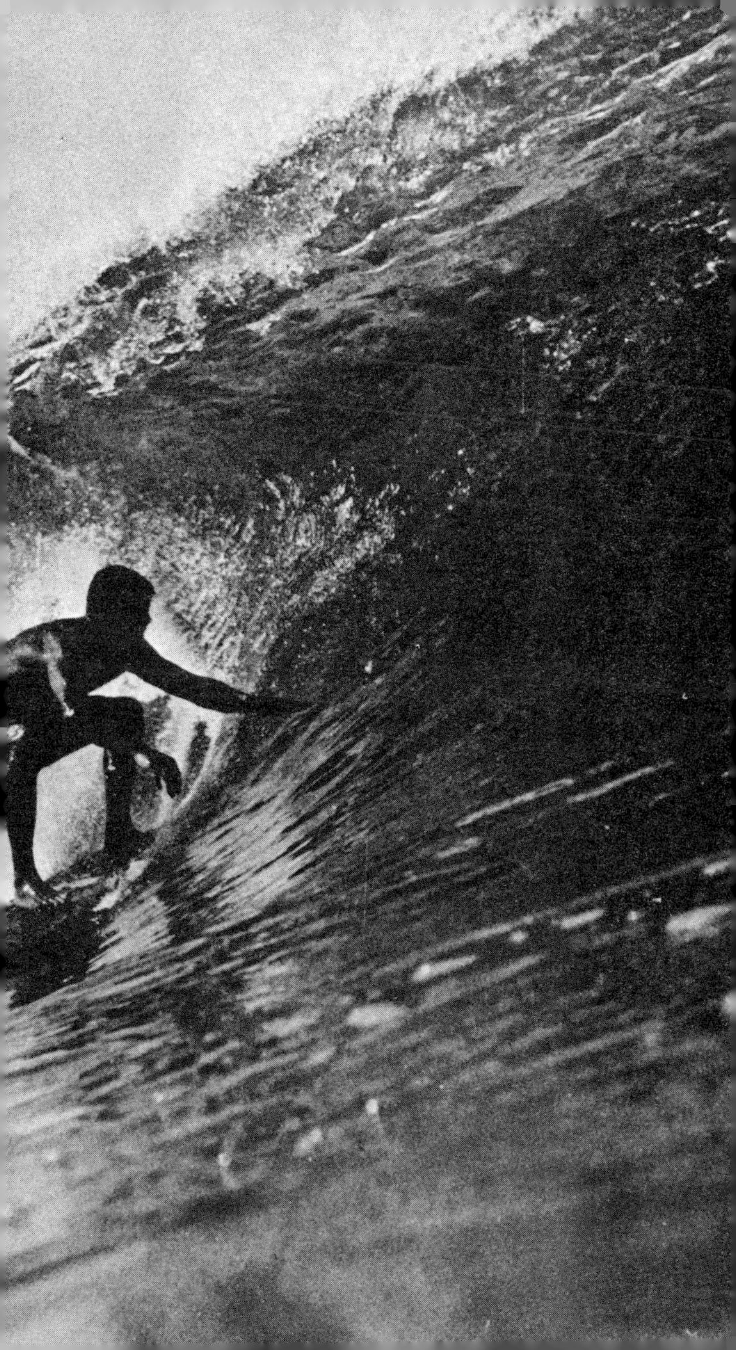

This photograph is of a political rally. Pretend that you went to the meeting. Imagine the colors of the balloons, the heat, the speeches, the cheers and clapping of the crowd.

Exercise 27:

Write a letter to a friend, describing your exciting experience as vividly as you can. Put your impressions into logical order, so that they form a *narrative*—a sequence or chain of events building up to an exciting *climax*.

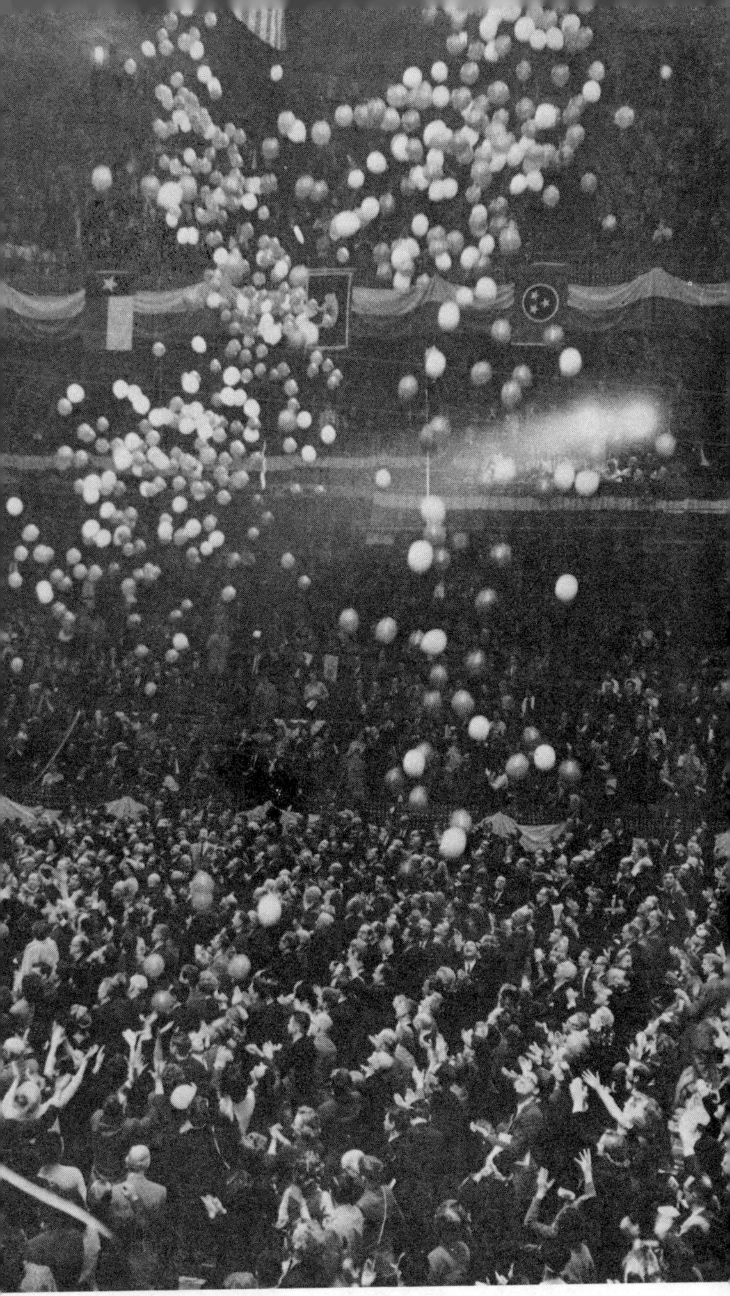

70

Choose this picture instead, if you prefer. Look at the upturned faces of the crowd. What are they looking at? Are they watching something frightening, or funny?

Exercise 28:

Pretend that you are a newspaper reporter who has come upon this scene. Write a news story for your paper, describing the event you think is taking place here. Answer quickly your readers' unspoken questions—Who? What? Where? When? Why? Then give the extra details. Keep your sentences short and sharp. Invent an eye-catching headline.

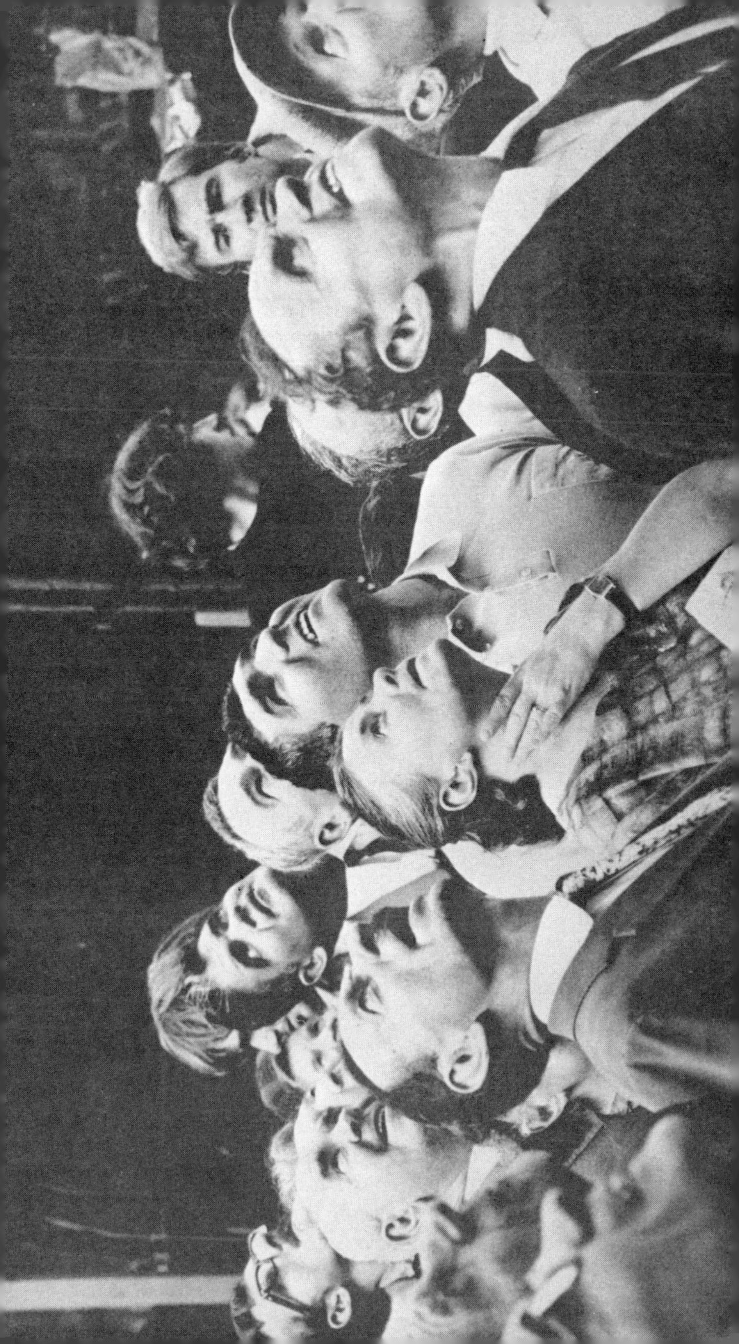

Pretend that you are an art critic for a newspaper or magazine.

Exercise 29:

You have seen the sculpture in an art show. Write a paragraph, describing the head for your readers. Try to tell them about the expression on the man's face. Why do you think the artist chose this man for his model? Who might the man be? What do you think the artist was trying to show? Tell your readers whether or not you like the sculpture.

73

Exercise 30:

This is a picture of Thailand (once called Siam), a small kingdom in southeast Asia.

Imagine that a society interested in geography and natural history has given you a travel grant, sending you to explore this place for a month. Your trip is now over. Write an interesting report for your sponsors, describing the weather, landscape, buildings, plants and animals, and how they impressed you. Include an imaginative account of the people, their customs and foods, if you like. (Your account does not have to be true, of course.) Try to give your account a clear beginning, middle and end.

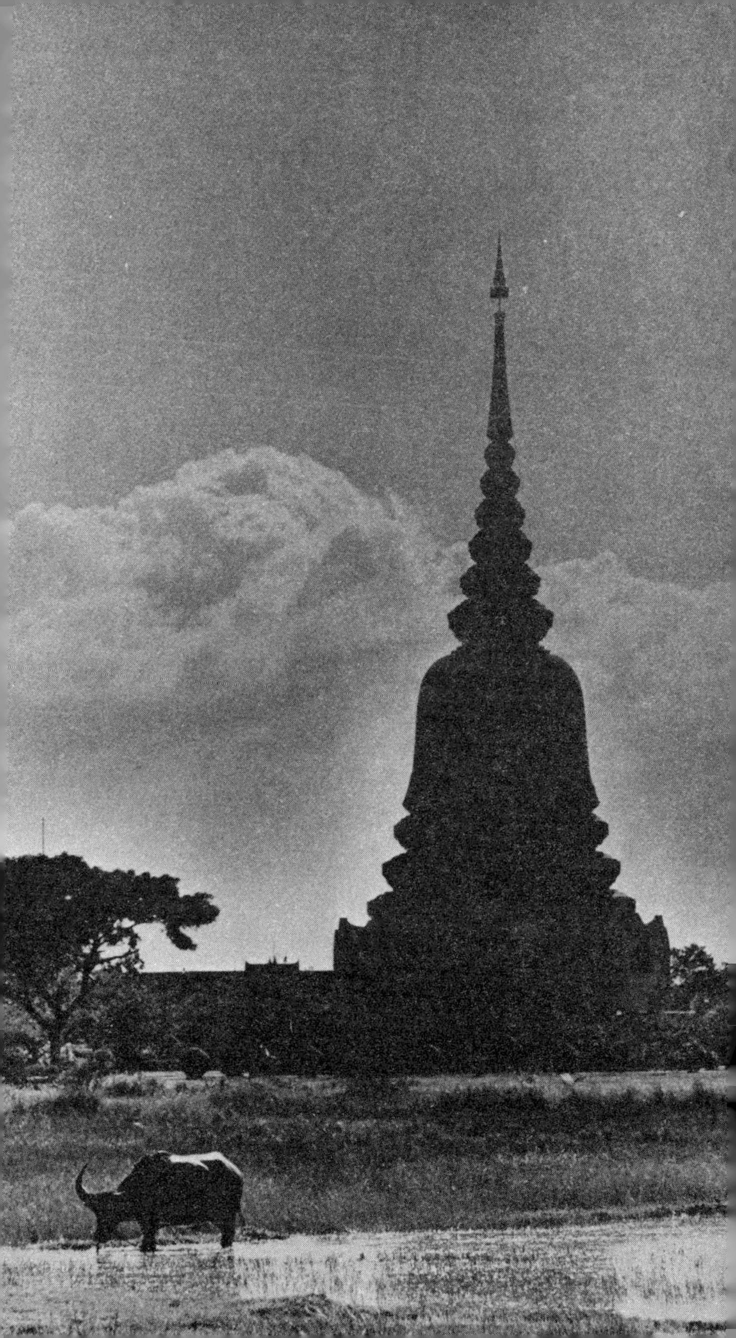

Look closely at this photograph. Can you see that the woman in the center is crying? Can you guess what is happening? These people are waiting, perhaps at the bottom of their own garden, to watch the funeral train of Robert Kennedy pass by. How do you think they feel?

Exercise 31:

Do you remember where you were, and what you were doing, when you heard that Robert Kennedy had been assassinated? People all over the world were shocked at the news. Pretend you have a friend who lives in Europe or South America. Write a letter to your friend, describing how you and the people around you felt when you heard the news. What did you all do? Why do you think he was shot? Use your imagination, if you like, as well as your memory. Arrange your letter into well-organized paragraphs, describing in order your actions, your emotions, what other people did, and your conclusions.

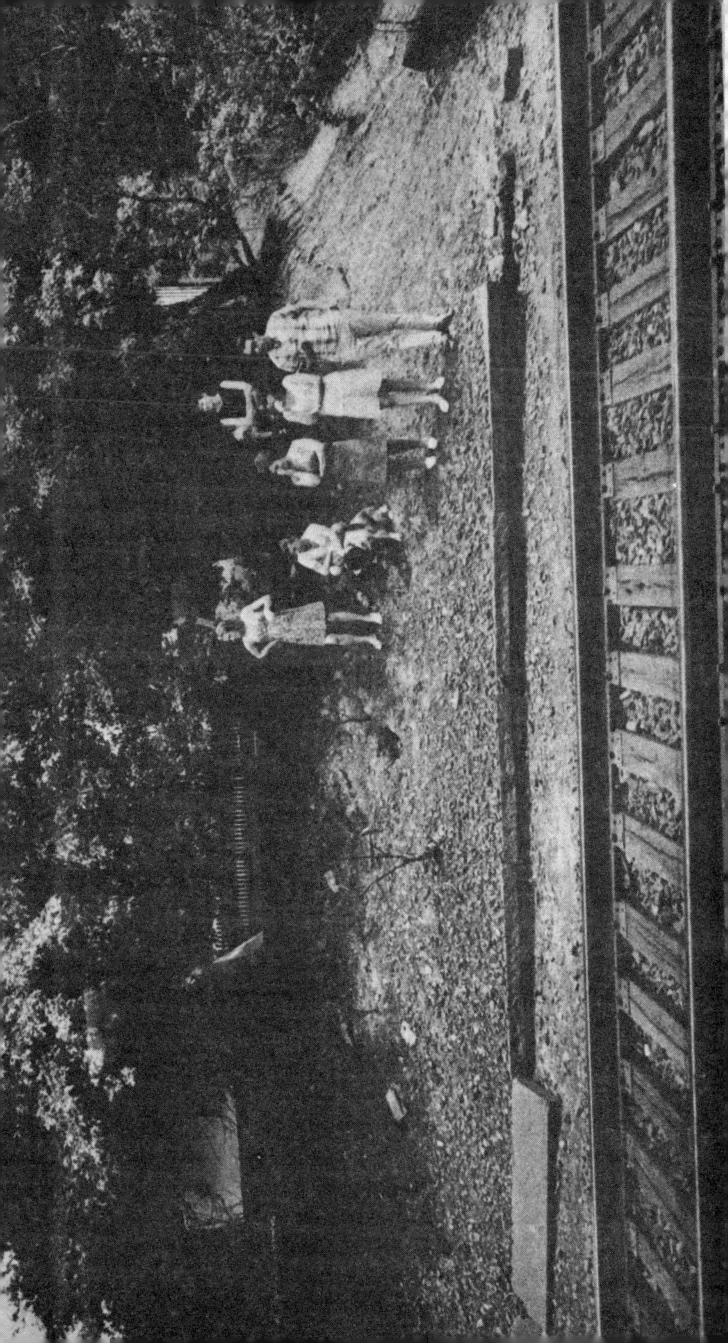

When you see a movie, you look at landscapes and rooms and objects that have been carefully chosen for effect. They provide the setting, and much of the mood, for the story. A Western, for example, might open with shots of a deserted ghost town, through which a lone gunman rides slowly. The camera might show you the empty saloon, its door swinging on one rusty hinge, and its grimy windows smashed. Dust covers everything. A mouse scuttles along the bar.

Exercise 32:

Pretend that you are working in Hollywood. You are writing the script for a new science-fiction movie about this strange being. (What is it? Where has it come from? What can it do with its unearthly powers?)

Write a "shot list," describing in order the scenes and objects to appear on the screen in the first few minutes of the film. They will set the mood. You can make your film frightening, if you like. Try to make the images as vivid as if they were on a screen in front of the reader's eyes. Explain when the cameraman moves the camera slowly across a wide landscape, or shoots a close-up of one small object.

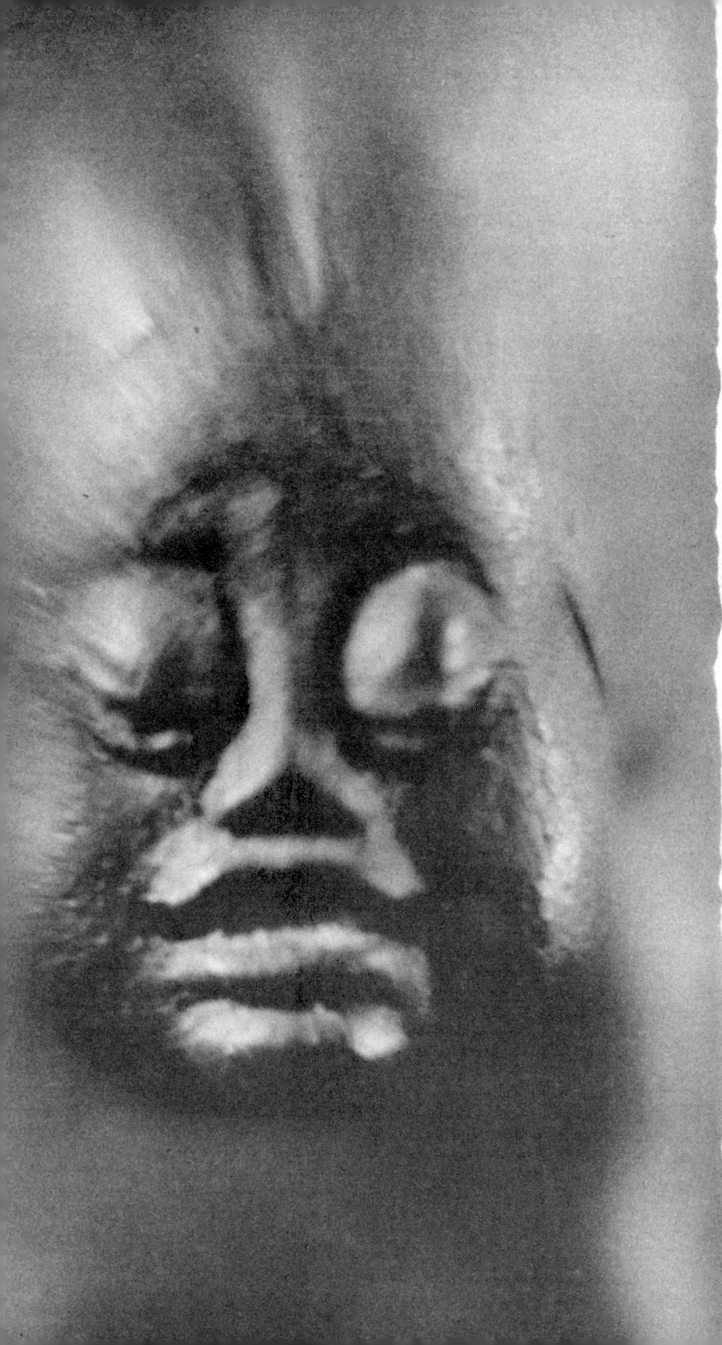

Alternate Exercise 32a:

Choose this picture, if you prefer. Look closely at the old man and the girl. (How does he earn his living? Is she his daughter? Are they happy?) Imagine the surroundings they live in, and describe the opening shots of a film about them. Set an unmistakable mood—your movie might be a love story, or a mystery. There is nothing in the picture to stop you making it an historical adventure, set a hundred years ago.

If your imagination spins out a whole plot about either of these pictures, don't stop... Carry on and write the whole movie.

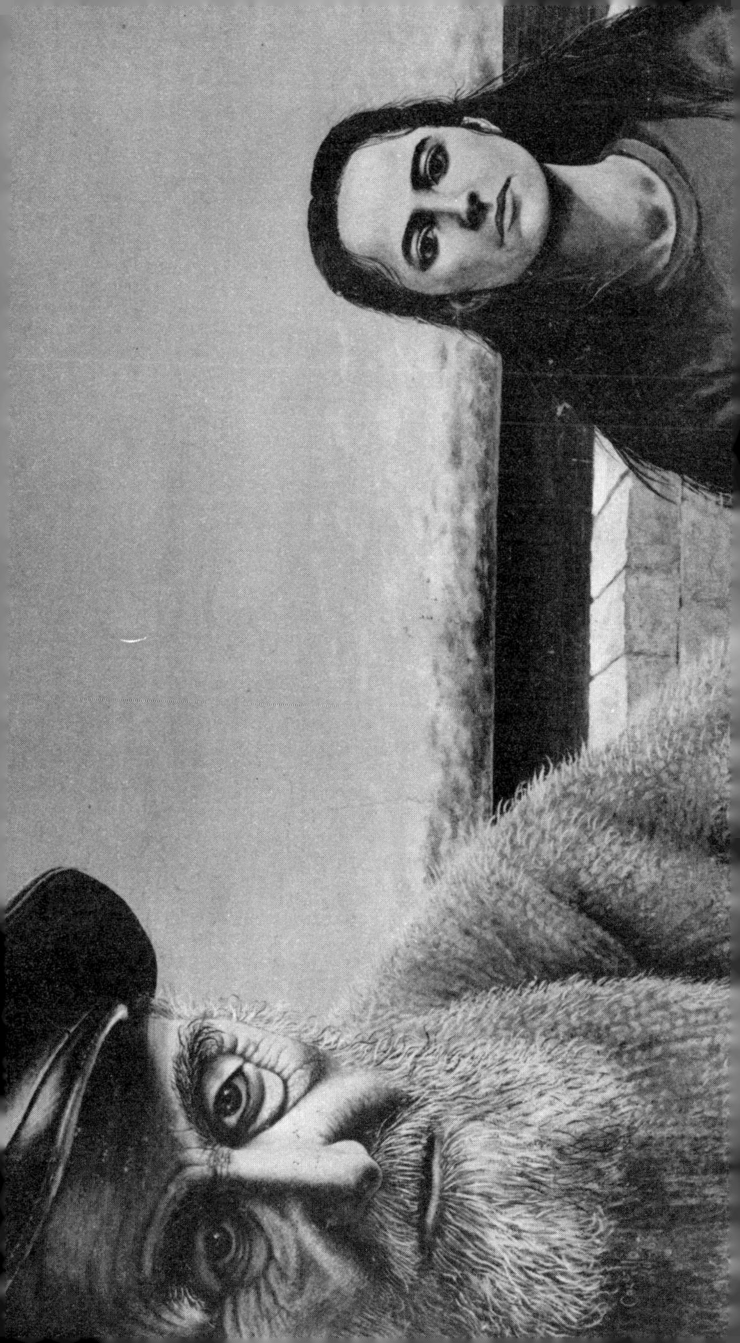

People

Interesting writing is usually about interesting people. A short-story writer often establishes a setting and mood just as an introduction to his main character— a person who will do, say or think something interesting. When you have enjoyed a talk with friends, too, you will notice that it has usually been about people who interest you—or about yourselves.

Magazines, newspapers, movies, television shows, plays, novels and short stories—without people in them, all these would disappear. Readers and viewers would no longer be interested in them. A good writer knows that people want to learn about other people. Gossip has always been one of mankind's favorite pastimes.

A writer learns to observe other people even more carefully than he looks at places and things.

If he is visiting real people in their home, or if he is beginning a piece of fiction, he may pay attention first to the rooms in which they live. A room or a house can often tell you a lot about its occupant. Is it clean and simply furnished, with fresh flowers? Or is it messy, and cluttered with dusty, fussy ornaments on every shelf and table?

Without ever seeing him, you know from his office that this art teacher is friendly, hospitable, trusting and generous—that he enjoys people and life—that he is punctual, and rather old-fashioned and sentimental:

Professor Gidney's door was always open even when he was teaching class somewhere else in the building, and in his studio were teacups and cookies and a hot plate which the students were free to use whenever they pleased. There was also a record player and a soft maple cabinet containing albums of operettas and waltzes: every afternoon punctually at five the music started.
—Evan S. Connell, Jr., "North Fayer Hall"

Physical appearance is interesting because it gives us so many clues to a person's character. The way a person decorates himself tells us how he feels about himself. We notice if a man has a full beard, how his hair is cut, and what clothes he wears. Is he conservative or eccentric? We notice a woman's make-up and hair. We look at her clothes and jewelry. Is she trying to attract other people's attention? Or has she chosen clothes that are unobtrusive, neat and functional?

Although it is not a hard and fast rule, many people use clothes, make-up and hair style to express their feelings about themselves. They may also wear certain styles to identify themselves with a social group they like.

Exercise 33:

Write four or five sentences describing this person. Describe everything the person is wearing, including accessories. Look at the hair. Explain how outer appearance gives clues to what sort of person this is. Look also at the face and the way of walking.

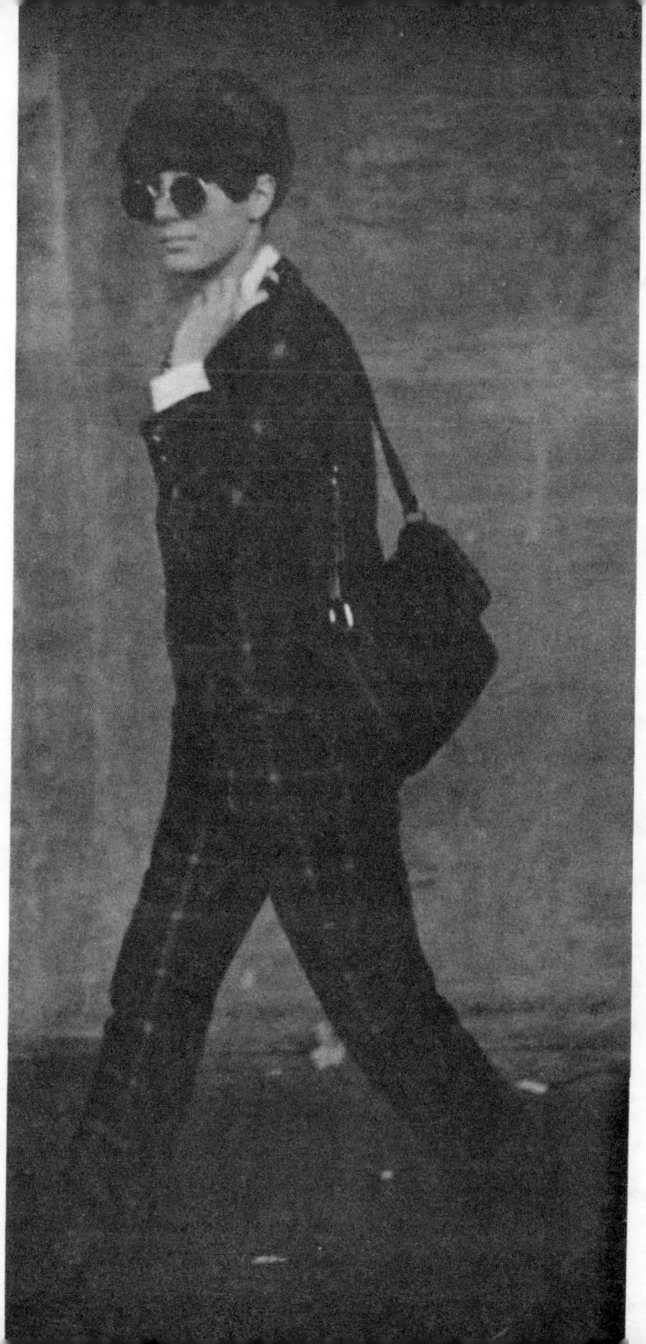

Good writers can describe a person in surprisingly few words. They are like target shooters with very accurate aim. Meet the hero of James Stephens' "Darling," who, significantly, is not even given a proper name.

> He had a long-haired thin-grown moustache. He had a large badly cut nose. He had dull blue eyes which stared, as tho' he were listening with them instead of with his ears. He had as little chin as could be without having no chin at all. His ears swung slightly outwards. The ends of his trousers flopped about his ankles, and from the flop and waggle of these garments one knew that his legs were as skinny as matchsticks.—(*Etched in Moonlight*)

In his story, "Rain," this is how Somerset Maugham describes a missionary's wife, a prim and rather self-righteous woman. Is she gentle? Is she tolerant of other people's weaknesses?

She was dressed in black and wore round her neck a gold chain, from which dangled a small cross. She was a little woman, with brown, dull hair very elaborately arranged, and she had prominent blue eyes behind invisible *pince-nez*. Her face was long, like a sheep's, but she gave no impression of foolishness, rather of extreme alertness; she had the quick movements of a bird. The most remarkable thing about her was her voice, high, metallic, and without inflection; it fell on the ear with a hard monotony, irritating to the nerves like the pitiless clamour of the pneumatic drill.

—Somerset Maugham, *Rain*

The photo on the next page shows only a small part of a man. But the picture contains enough clues for you to guess what kind of a person he may be.

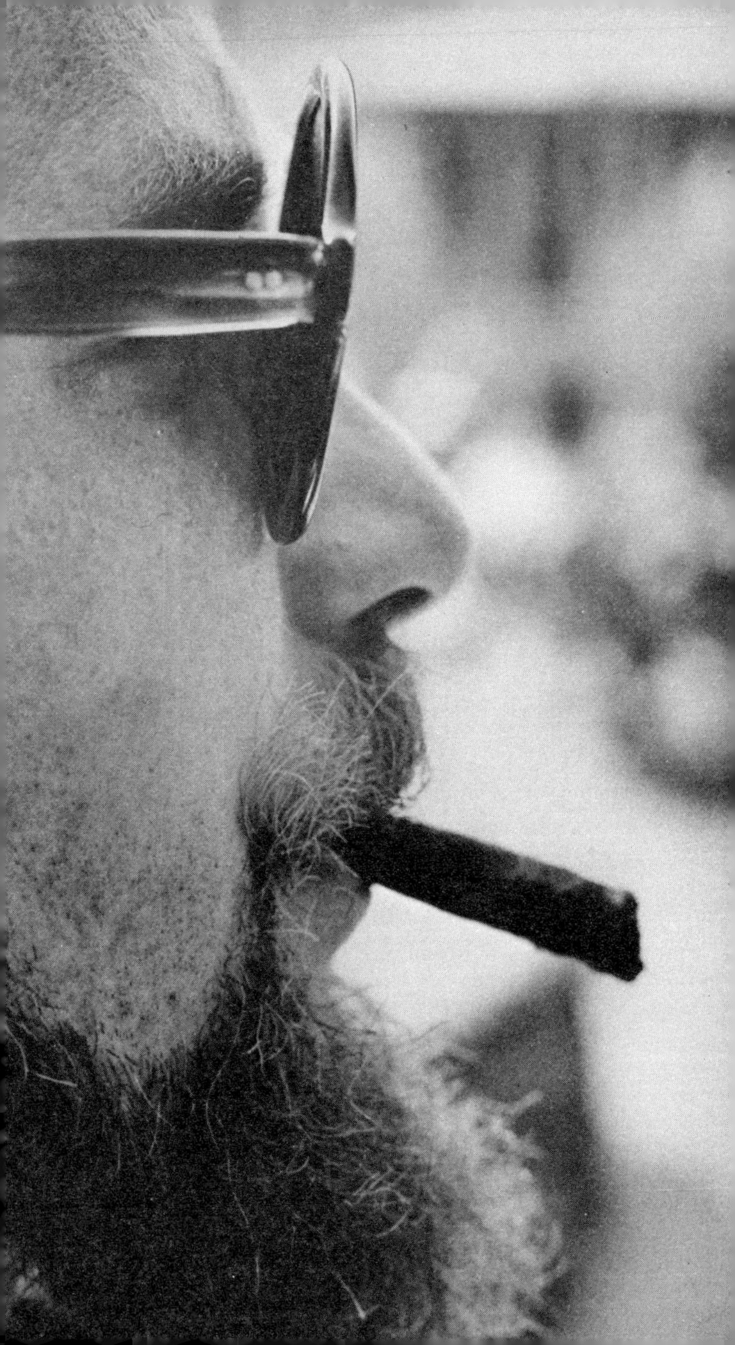

Exercise 34:

Write five or six sentences (or more) about this man's appearance and probable character. Describe what you see, and use the visible clues to deduce his personality. How old do you think the man is? How long has he had his beard? Are his sunglasses in style? What sort of expression does he have on his face? Would you say he was timid? Nervous? Self-satisfied? Serious? Evil? Self-conscious? Humble? Vain? Clever? Effeminate?

Character is what makes one person different from all others. Think about the most outstanding people you know. What makes them different from the crowd? Why is the most popular person you know singled out by the others? What qualities does that person have that most other people lack? Who is the oddball in your crowd—and why? Who is the most obnoxious person you have met? What makes that person disliked?

Each person you know has individual qualities. Even if he is not outstanding, there is no one else in the world quite like him. Ask yourself questions about people. Watch strangers. Look at their physical appearance, their expressions, their effect on others. Use a bit of imagination on what you have seen, and you will have material on enough interesting characters to fill many stories.

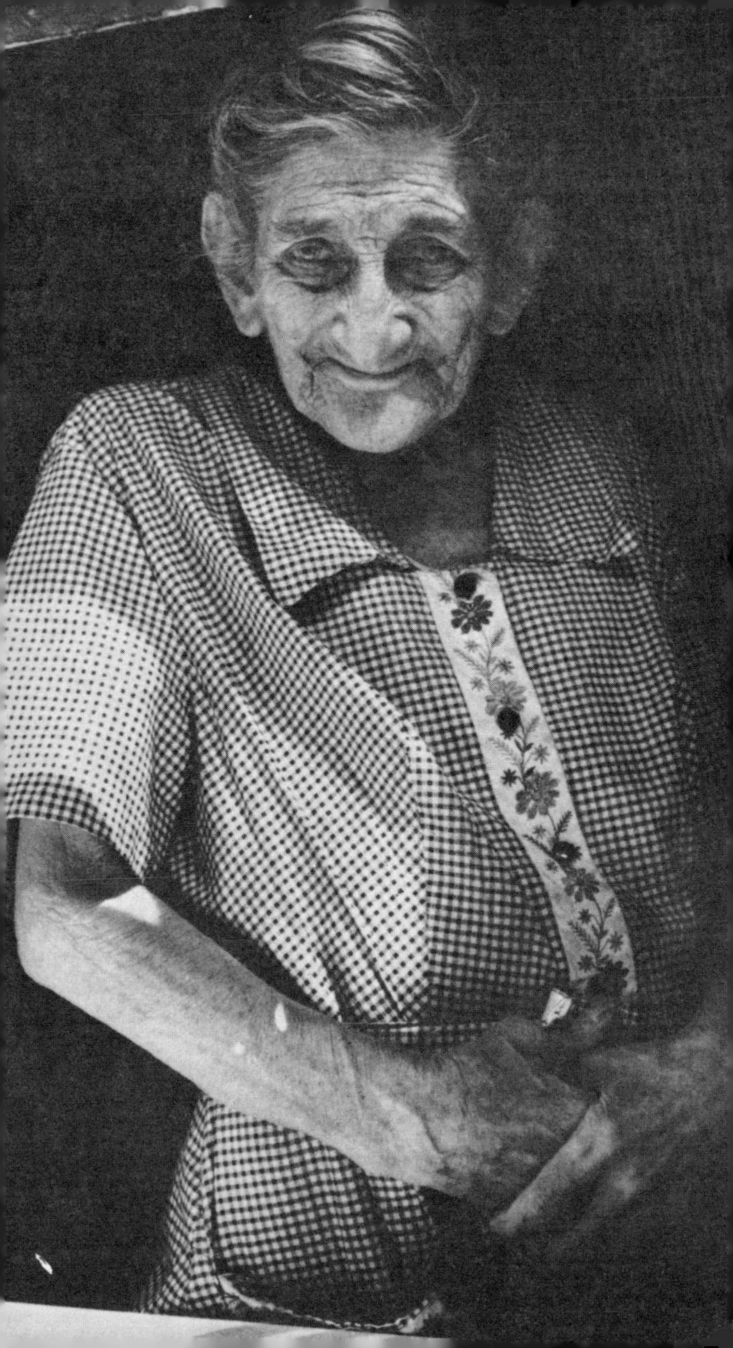

Exercise 35:

Write half a page, or more, about the appearance and character of the old woman. Look carefully at her hands, hair and dress. Does she look happy? Would her home be neat and cheerful, or dusty and dark? Use your imagination to make up a short account of her past life, and some of her present activities and habits.

Temporary expressions pass over a person's face and tell you about his emotions and thoughts. Most people find it difficult to be "inscrutable," to prevent their faces from showing what they are feeling or thinking. This is especially true with very strong emotions, such as rage or panic, shown by extreme facial expressions as well as actions.

A writer learns to look also for expressions that are subtle, not obvious. Sometimes an expression may fool you, but it is always worth watching. A slight smile may show pleasure, scorn or amusement. A frown may reveal displeasure—or simply a reaction to bright sunlight.

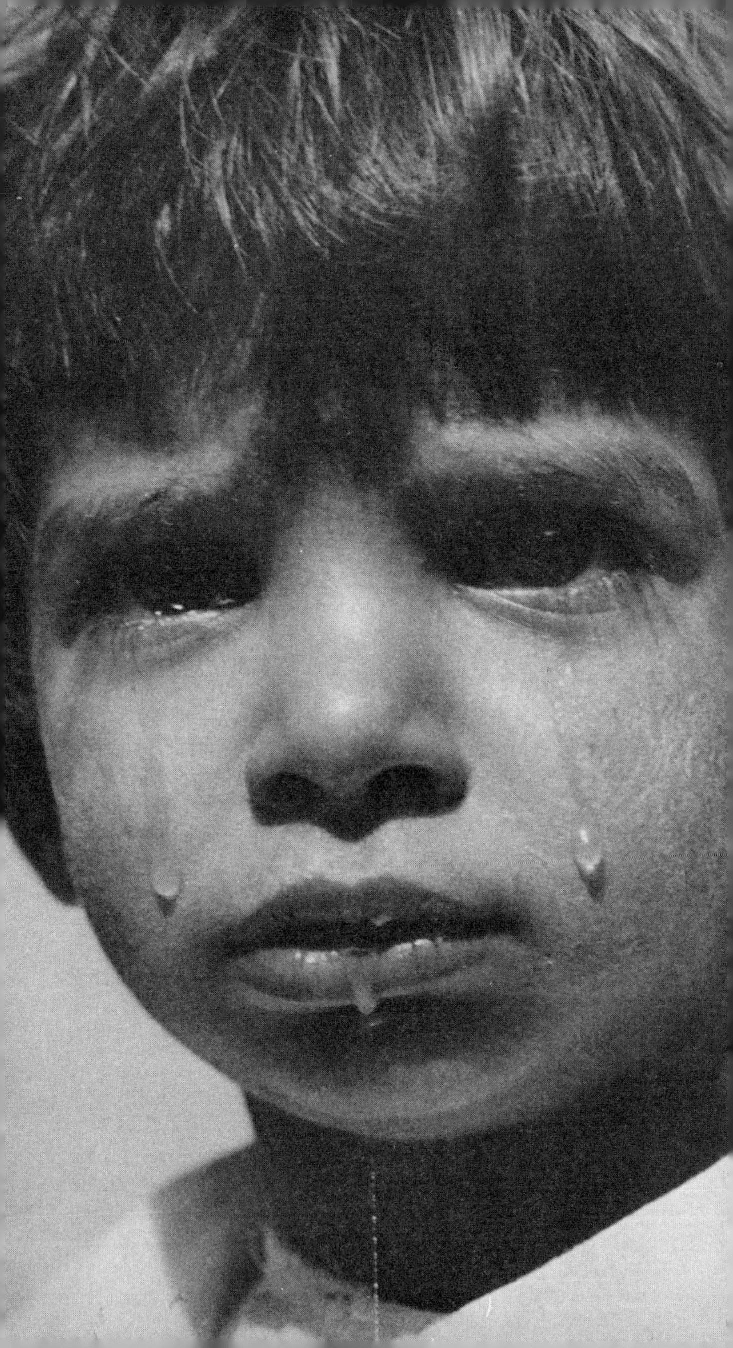

Exercise 36:

The expression on the little girl's face leaves no doubt about what she is feeling. Notice her eyes and lips particularly. Write four or five sentences, describing the way her emotions are registered on her face.

A writer often describes expressions on characters' faces to make the events in a story vivid. It is a way of letting the reader draw his own conclusions, without the person of the author intruding to tell him what to think. Katherine Mansfield describes a chance meeting between a woman and a man she hadn't seen for six years. See how effective it is to show us their expressions, instead of just saying that the man didn't recognize the woman at first:

> He must have felt that shock of recognition in her for he looked up and met her eyes. Incredible! He didn't know her! She smiled; he frowned. She came towards him. He closed his eyes an instant, but opening them his face lit up as though he had struck a match in a dark room. He laid down the orange and pushed back his chair....
> —Katherine Mansfield, *Bliss*

Exercises 37 and 38:

Write half a page each about the two women on the next pages. Describe their appearance (clothes, hair, age, neatness). Use as many adjectives as you can to describe their apparent emotions. Make the two women as different as possible from one another. If you like, give a brief, imaginative account of what has happened to cause their expressions.

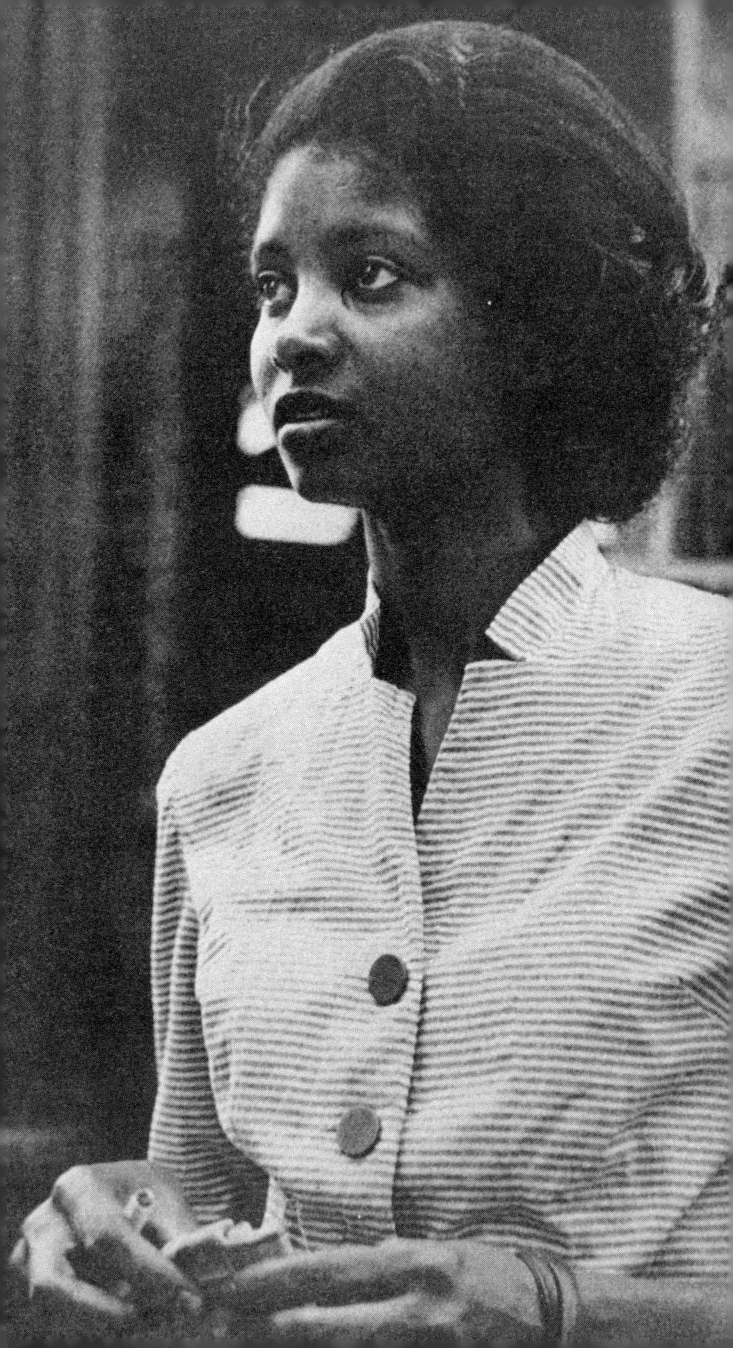

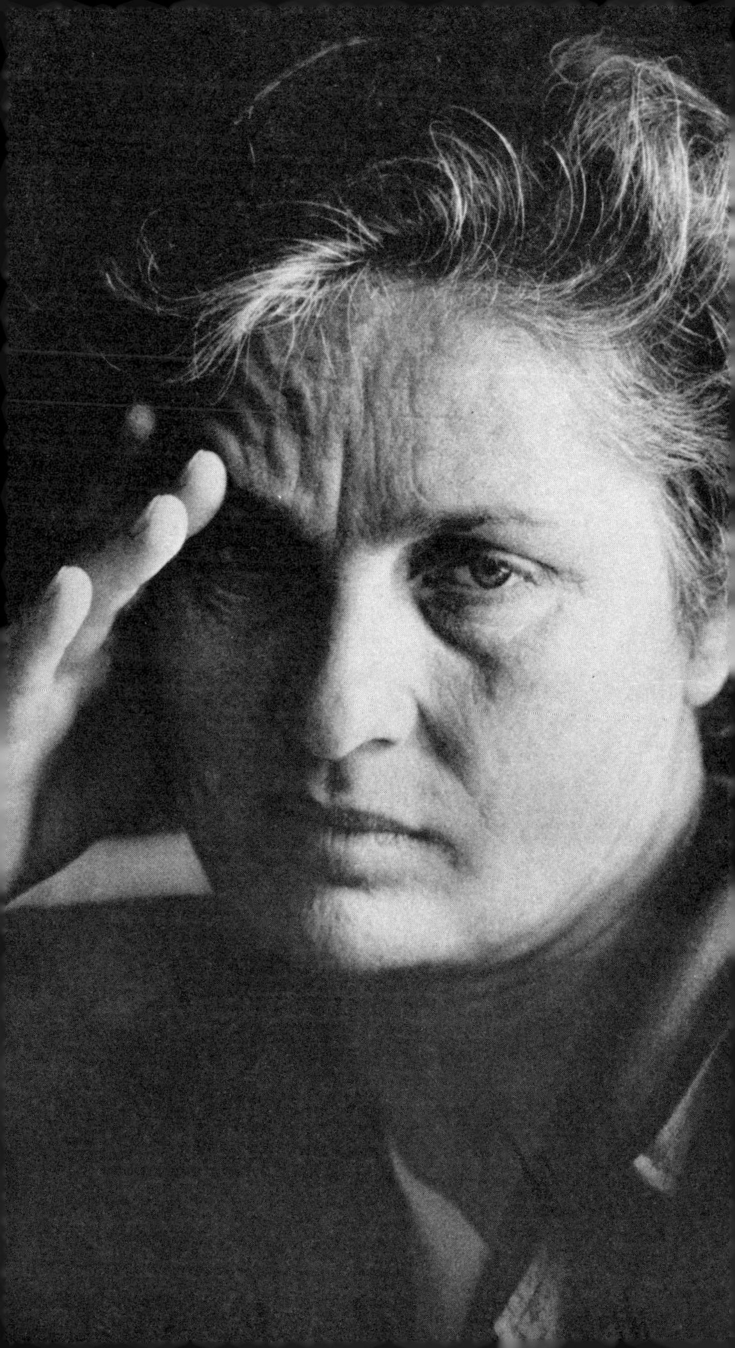

Exercise 39:

The boy on this page was photographed in a portrait studio in 1860, just before he left to fight for the Confederates in the Civil War. The expression on his face is subtle. Write half a page, describing his appearance and his expression as it appears to you. How old do you think he is? Is he afraid? Who is the portrait for? Try to give some account of thoughts running through his mind as he waits for the photographer to take his picture.

97

Alternate Exercise 39a:

This boy lives in India. He helps his large family by selling melons in the marketplace. His hard life would not satisfy many of us. Write half a page about his appearance and expression. Is he happy? What sort of daily life do you think he leads? What does he enjoy?

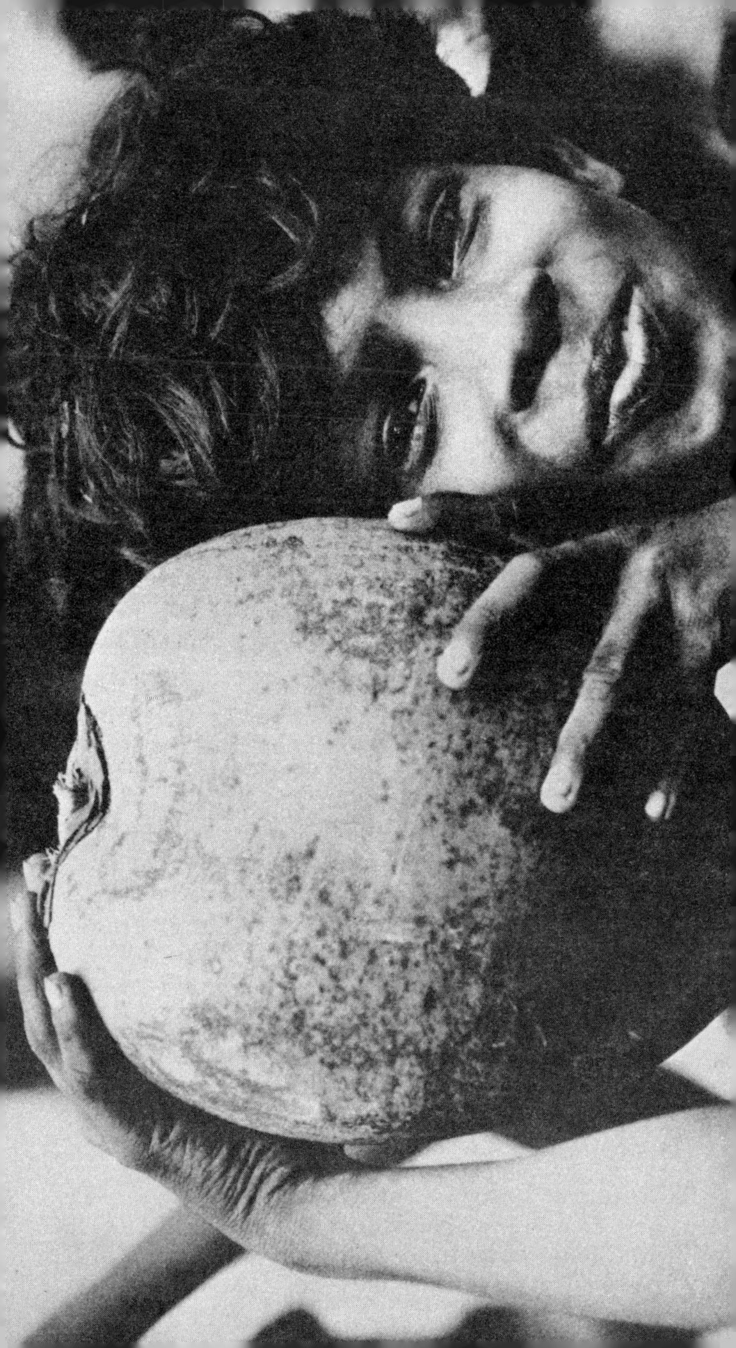

The expressions on a person's face are usually reinforced by other parts of his body. Notice the way a man holds his head or twitches his hands, the way he slouches or shuffles, his general "manner." In *Winesburg, Ohio*, Sherwood Anderson writes about a short, fat old man whose most noticeable feature was his hands:

Wing Biddlebaum talked much with his hands. The slender expressive fingers, forever active, forever striving to conceal themselves in his pockets or behind his back, came forth and became the piston rods of his machinery of expression.

The story of Wing Biddlebaum is the story of hands. Their restless activity, like ... the beating of the wings of an imprisoned bird, had given him his name. Some obscure poet of the town had thought of it. The hands alarmed their owner. He wanted to keep them hidden away and looked with amazement at the quiet inexpressive hands of other men who worked beside him in the fields, or passed, driving sleepy teams on country roads.
—Sherwood Anderson, *Winesberg, Ohio*

The picture of the musician is not a static portrait. The man is caught in action—moving, concentrating on the music that means so much to him.

Exercise 40:

Write half a page, or more, about the musician. Describe his appearance, the expression on his face, the movements of his hands and body. Try to guess at his personality. (Include sounds, too, if you like.)

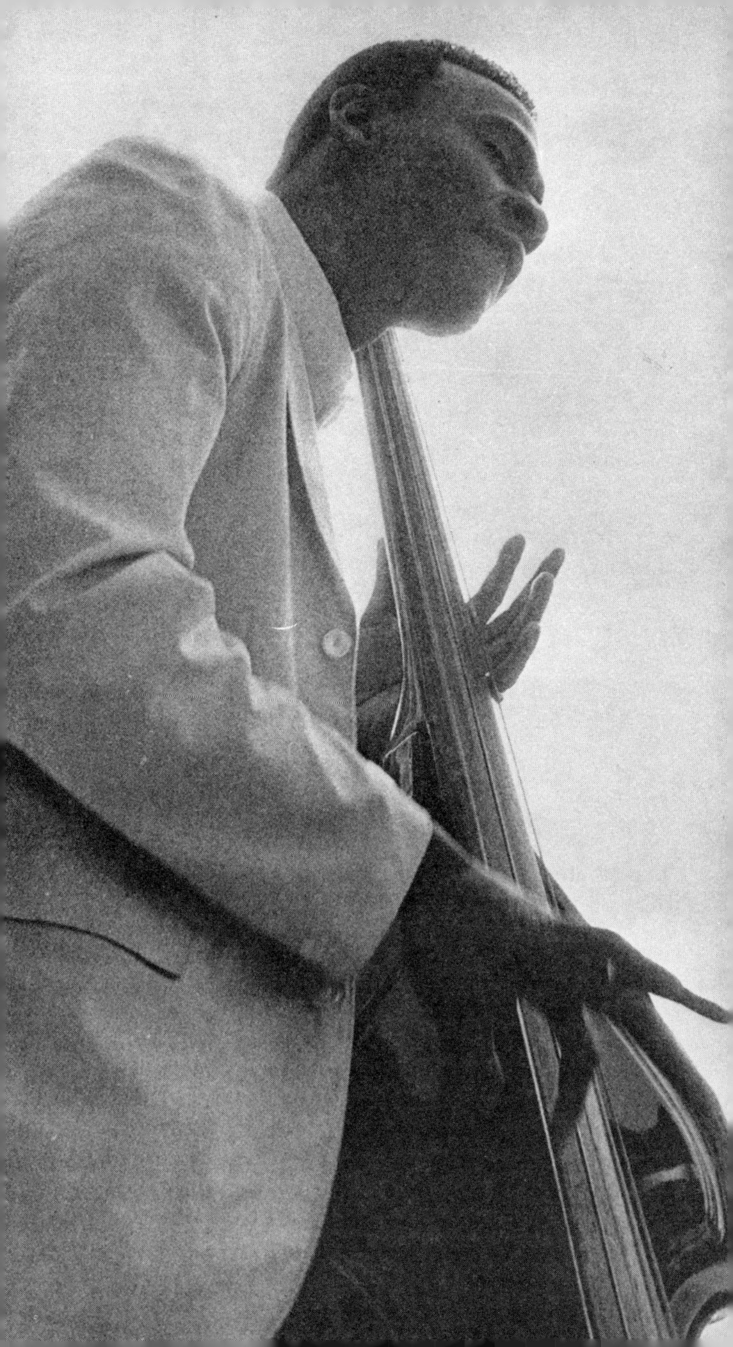

The photo of the woman gives you a chance to combine all the techniques you have learned in this chapter.

Exercise 41:

Write one page, or more, about the woman and this scene. Describe all the details of her outer appearance—her clothes, accessories, hair—using them as clues to her personality. What sort of character does she have? Do you like her? How old is she? Describe the expression on her face, and the way in which she is walking past the men. What is she thinking? Make up a short account of her past life, to explain her present appearance and emotional attitude.

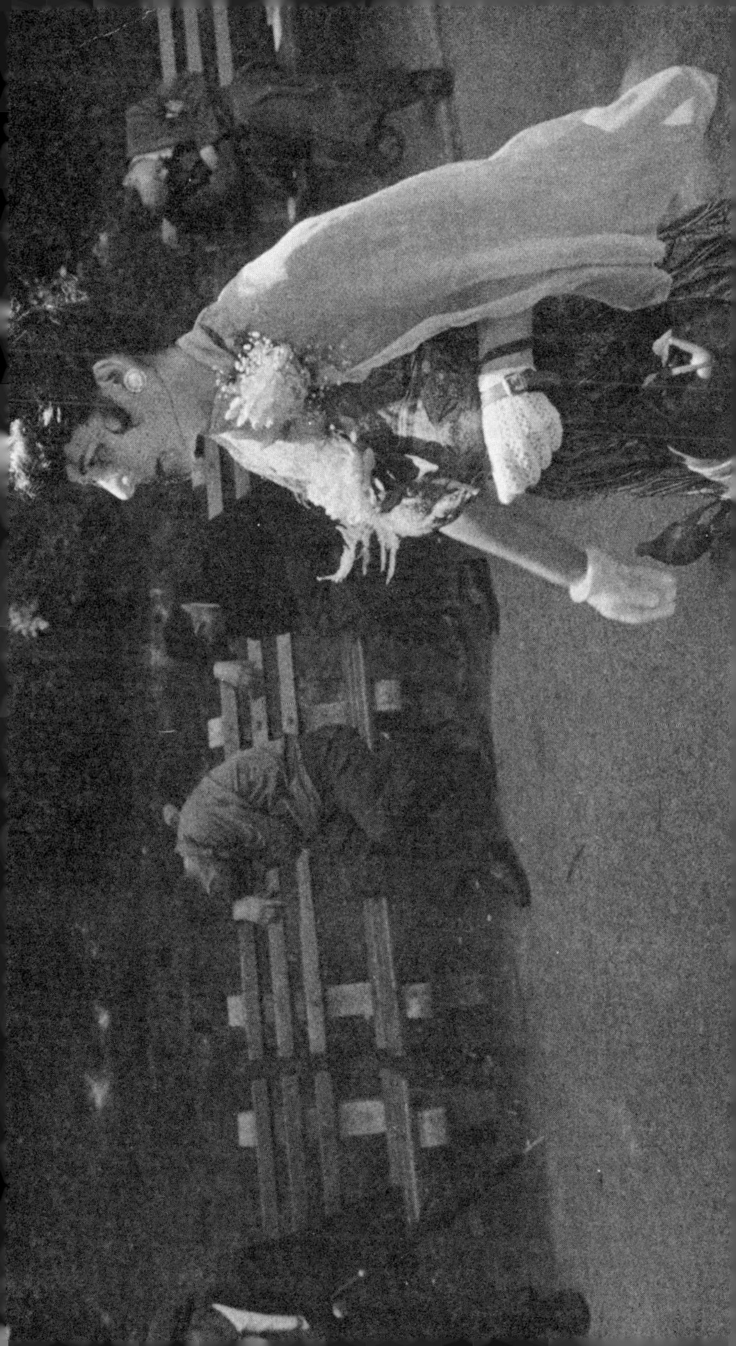

Point
Of
View

In the chapter on scene and mood, you saw that the way a place looks can vary with the observer's mood. It is also true that places and events always look slightly different to all people because of differences in their personalities. No two spectators will tell you exactly the same things about an event. Because of their own character and outlook on life, they will think some aspects are more important than others. They will interpret what they see in different ways. They will remember different details.

An extreme example of a personal view of the world can be found in William Faulkner's novel *The Sound and the Fury*. A large part of this book is written as if from the viewpoint of Benjy, a man with the mind of a three-year-old child, who cannot even talk. This is how he sees the garden, and girls who remind him of his lost sister:

... Our shadows were on the grass. They got to the trees before we did. Mine got there first. Then we got there, and then the shadows were gone. There was a flower in the bottle. I put the other flower in it.

... I went down to the gate, where the girls passed with their booksatchels. They looked at me, walking fast, with their heads turned. I tried to say, but they went on, and I went along the fence, trying to say, and they went faster. Then they were running and I came to the corner of the fence and I couldn't go any further, and I held to the fence, looking after them and trying to say.
—William Faulkner, *The Sound and the Fury*

This photograph of an Italian family was taken at Ellis Island in 1905. They are immigrants who have just landed from their ship, looking for their lost luggage.

Exercise 42:

From the view point of either the mother or her son, describe the confusing scene in front of their eyes. Write down the observer's own thoughts and emotions about what he or she sees. The thoughts can wander to the past (in Italy or on the ship), or to the future (in America), if you like. Make the point of view in your writing so clear that you don't have to label it "Mother" or "Son." If you prefer, you can try writing through the eyes of one of the little girls.

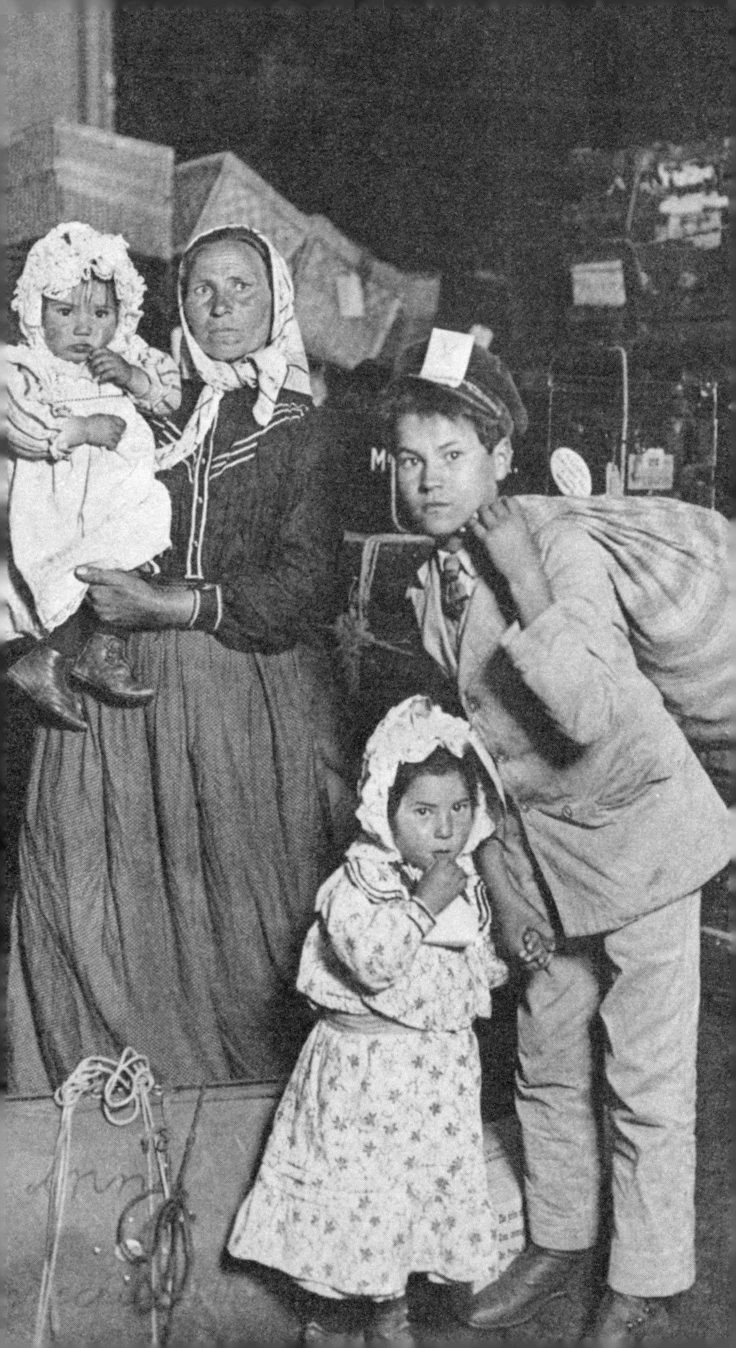

Exercise 43:

Write half a page (or more), describing the sights and sounds of the bus station from the viewpoint of one of the people in the picture. You might choose the boy with his chin in his hands, or the man in the white cap. Try to make the person's character, as well as his temporary mood, show through the description. Explain why he is there, and reproduce some of his thoughts and feelings.

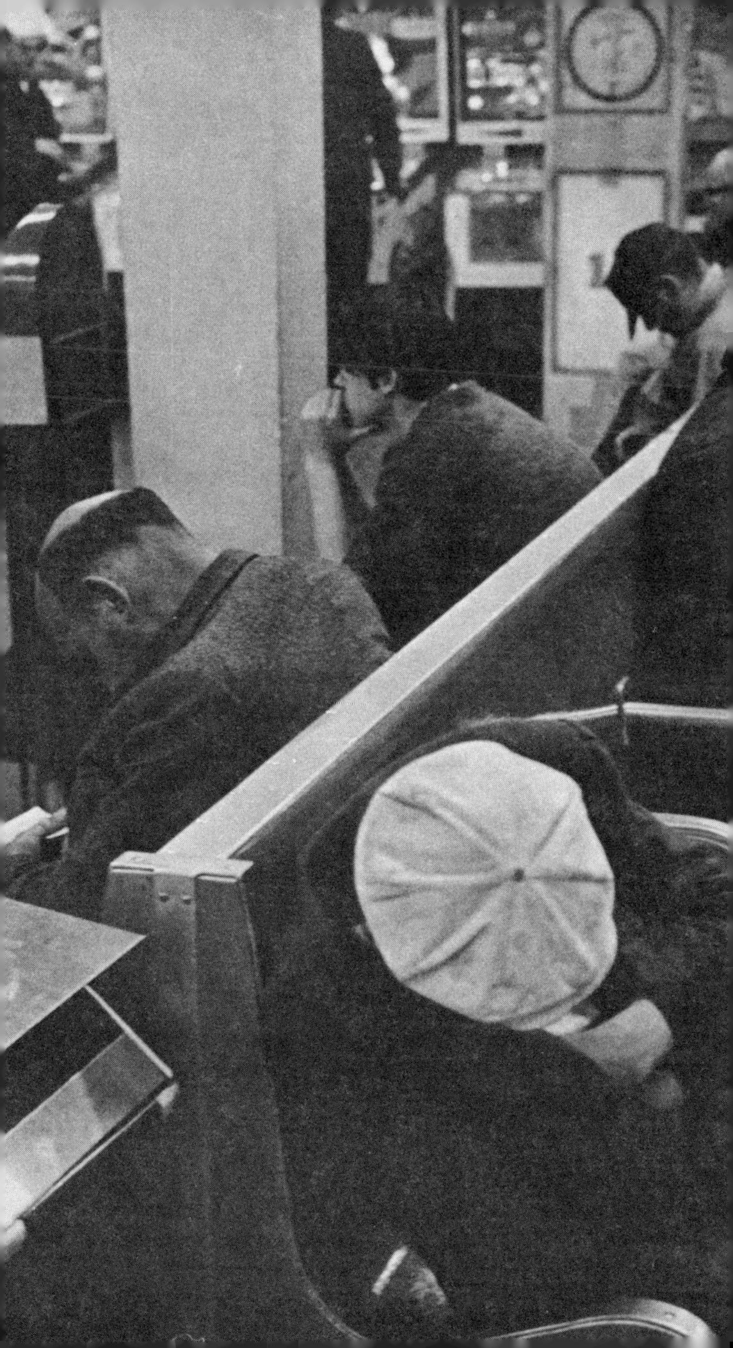

In the next three pictures, there is an emotional difference or barrier between the people in them, causing their viewpoints to vary. In the first picture, this barrier is the age difference between the child and her grandmother. In the second, it is the authority of the school. In the third, it is the difference in sex between the two girls and the boy.

Exercises 44 and *45*:

Choose two out of the three pictures. Write a page on each of your two choices. Describe what is happening from both the point of view of the teacher *and* student, or girls *and* boy, or grandmother *and* child. In the first picture, for example, the old lady may be thinking of the past, while the child is living only in the present. Explain people's thoughts and feelings. Try to give the people some clear personality. Explain why they are there.

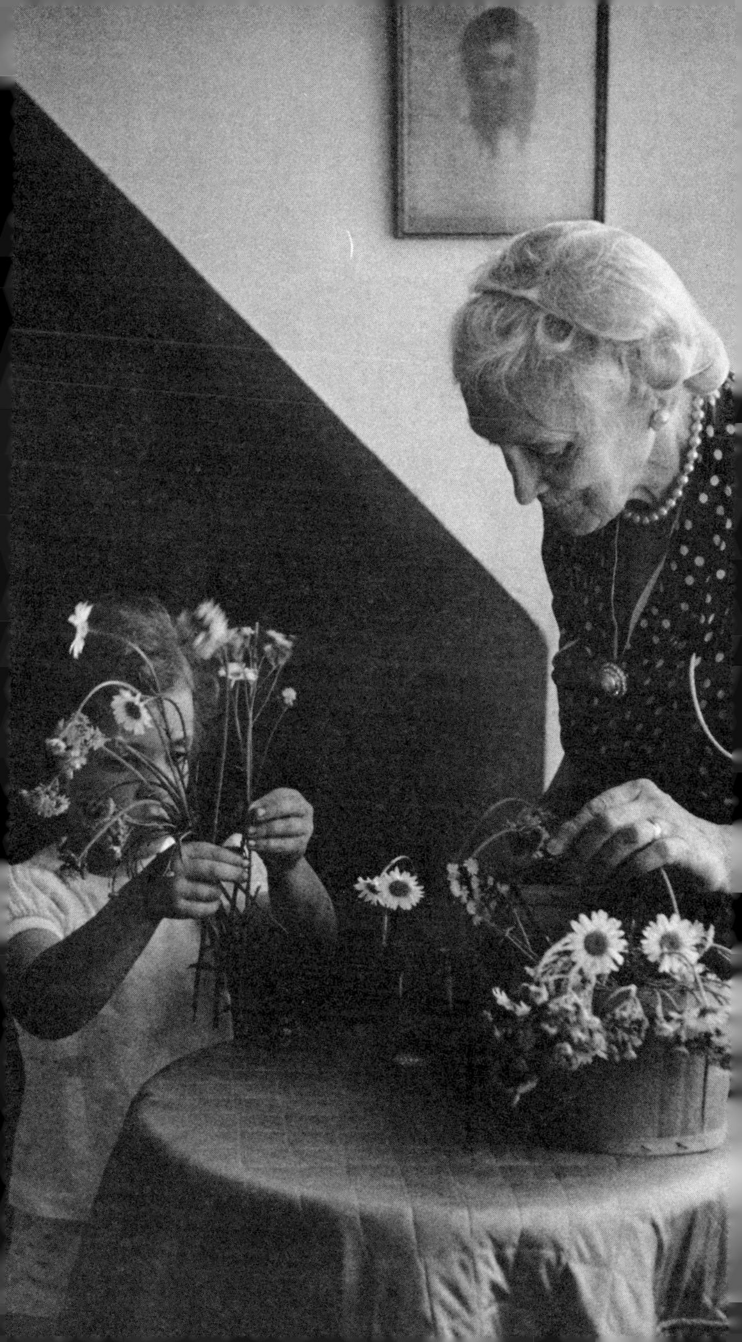

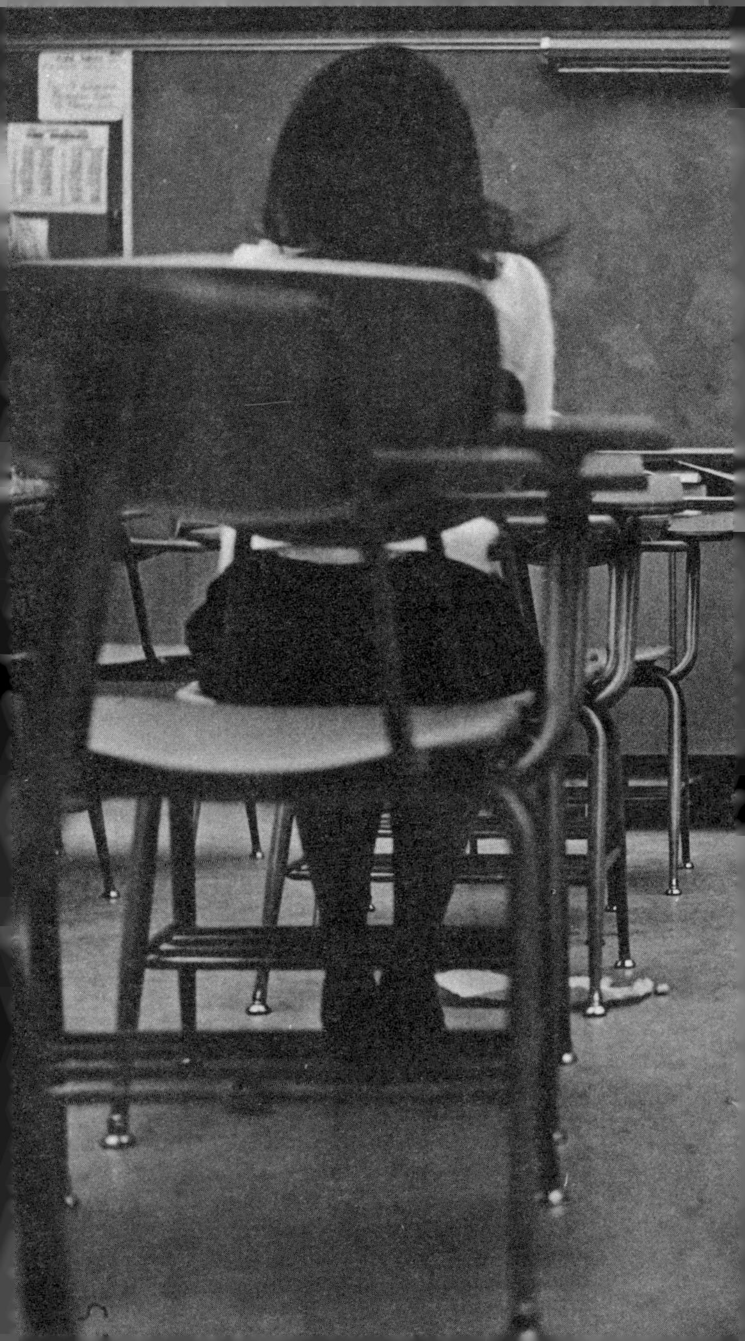

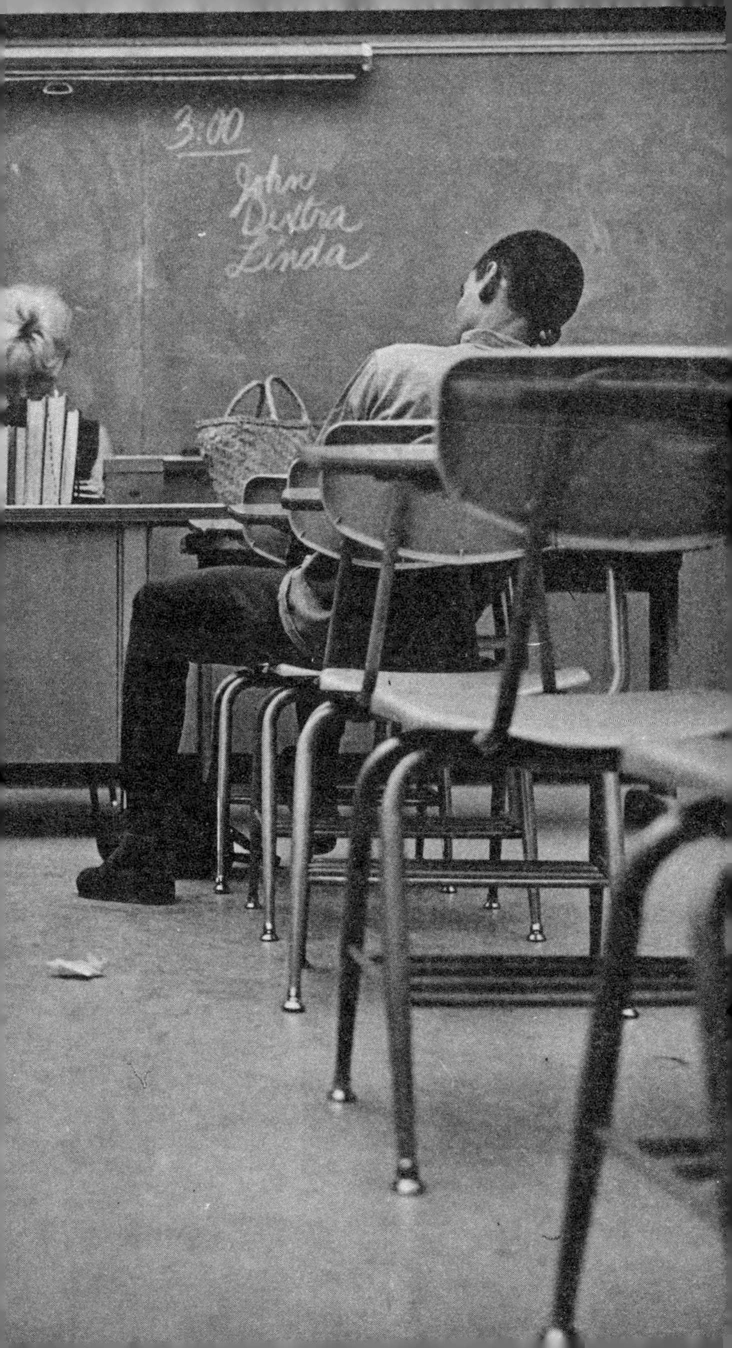
3:00
John
Dixtra
Linda

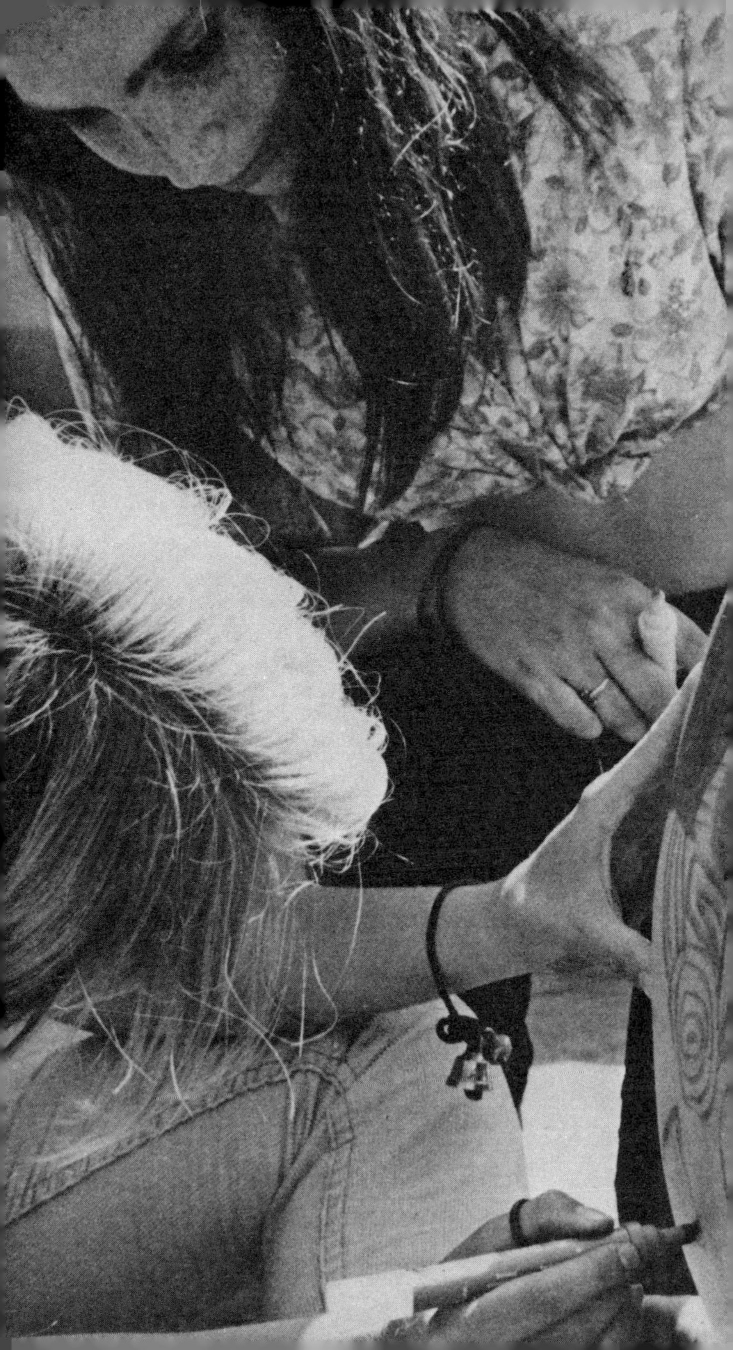

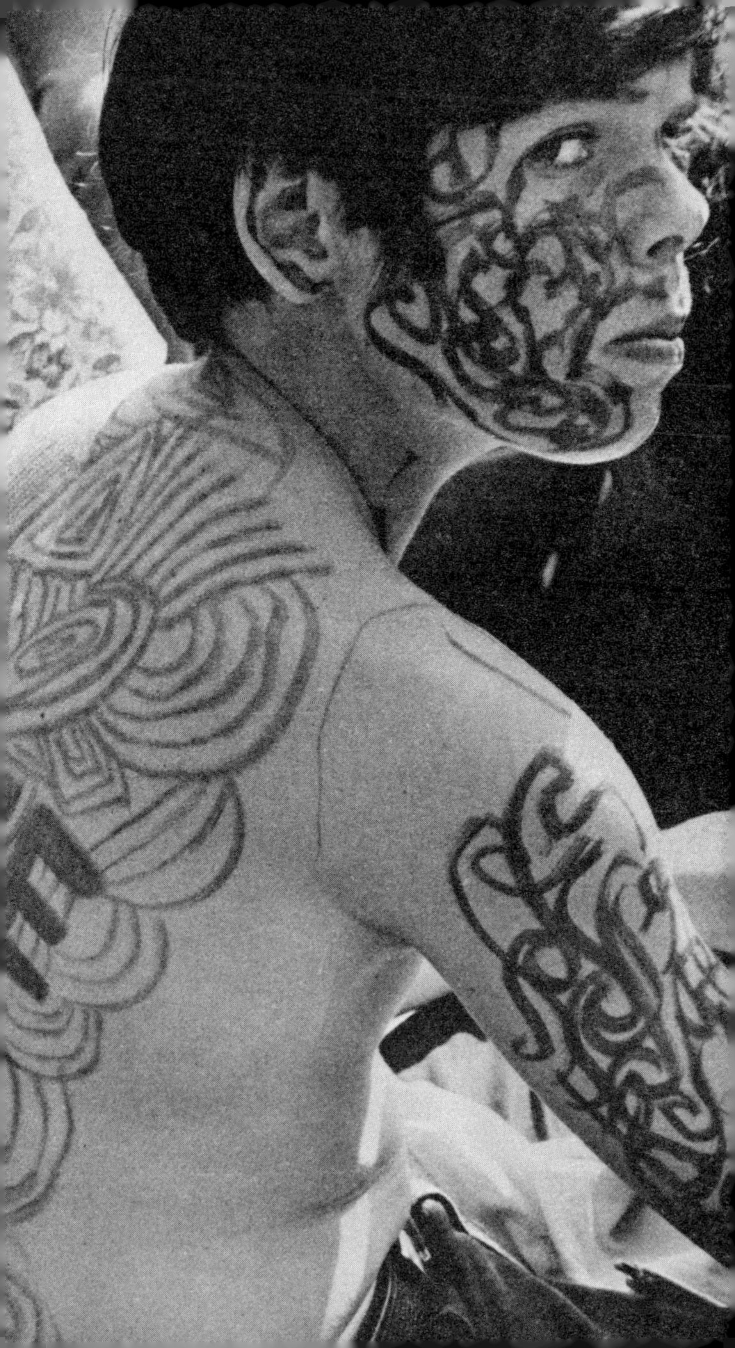

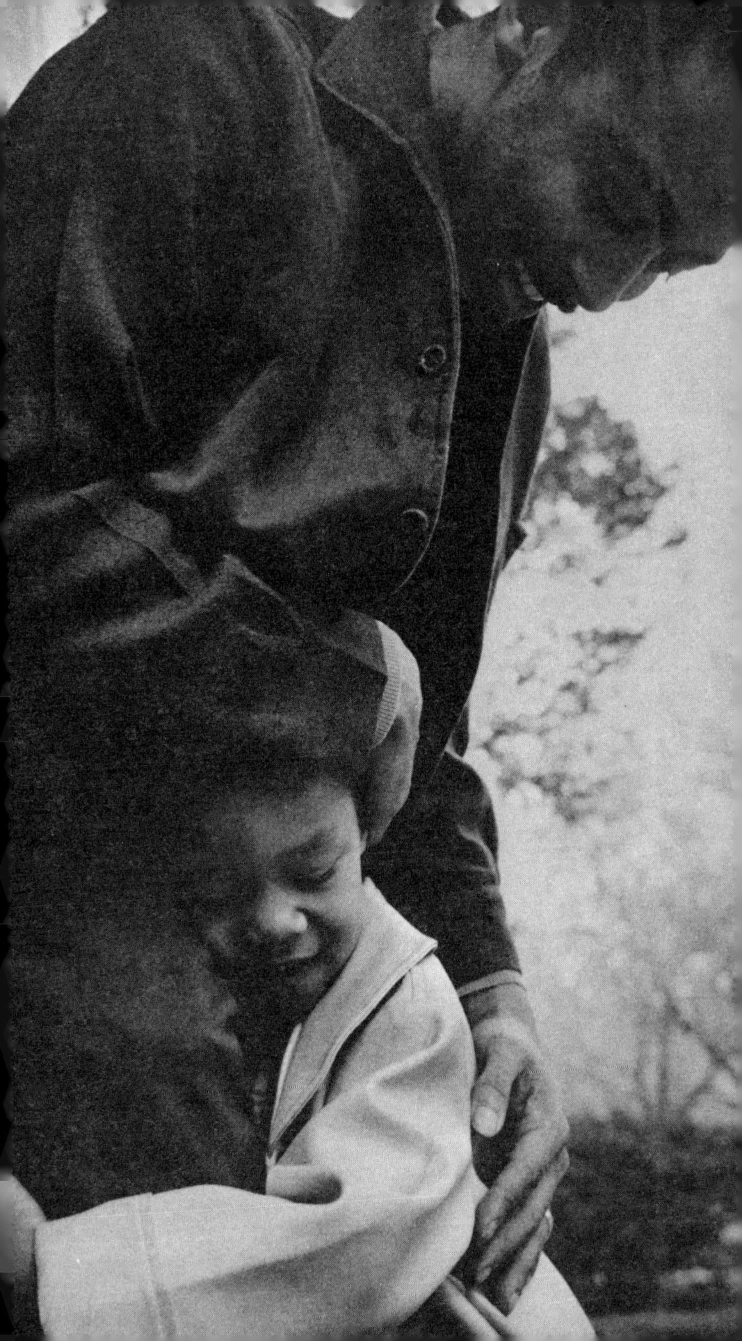

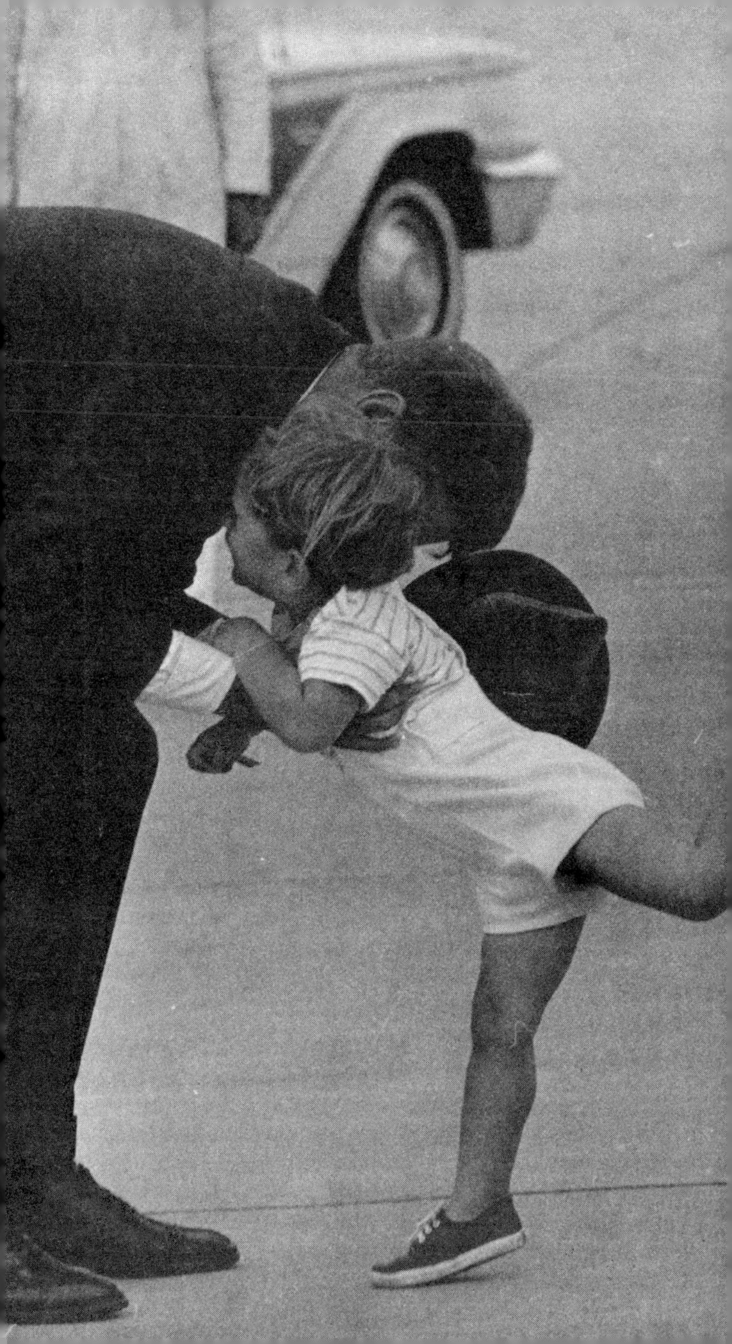

118

The two photos of fathers and children on the preceding pages are superficially alike. But there is an emotional difference between the two scenes. The difference is partly caused by circumstances—one father has just got off the plane from a trip, while the other is taking his daughter for a walk in the park.

Exercise 46:

Write at least a page about these two scenes. Put yourself in the place of the four people, one by one, and write about quarter of a page describing one person's emotions and thoughts. Make each of the four people as different as possible from one another. Do you recognize one of the fathers?

Exercise 47:

Look carefully at the picture on the next page. Choose one of the people in the crowd watching the parade. Write about this person, in a two-part exercise. In Part 1, using the techniques you practiced in the chapter on people, describe the person's physical appearance and probable personality, as they strike you as an "outside" observer. In Part 2, move "inside" the person. Write a paragraph of thoughts and emotions (and memories, perhaps) the person has while watching the parade. Make your readers see the parade through the person's eyes.

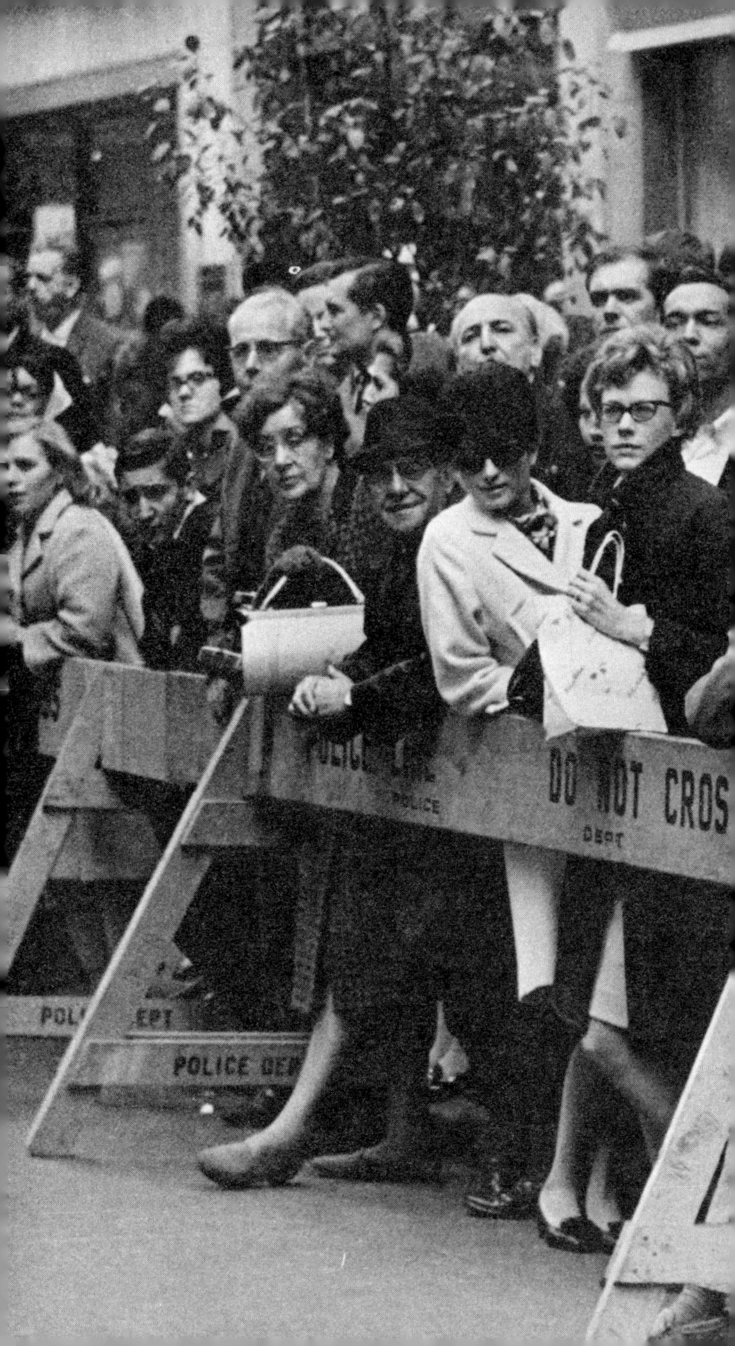
DO NOT CROS
DEPT
POLICE
POLICE DEP
POL EPT

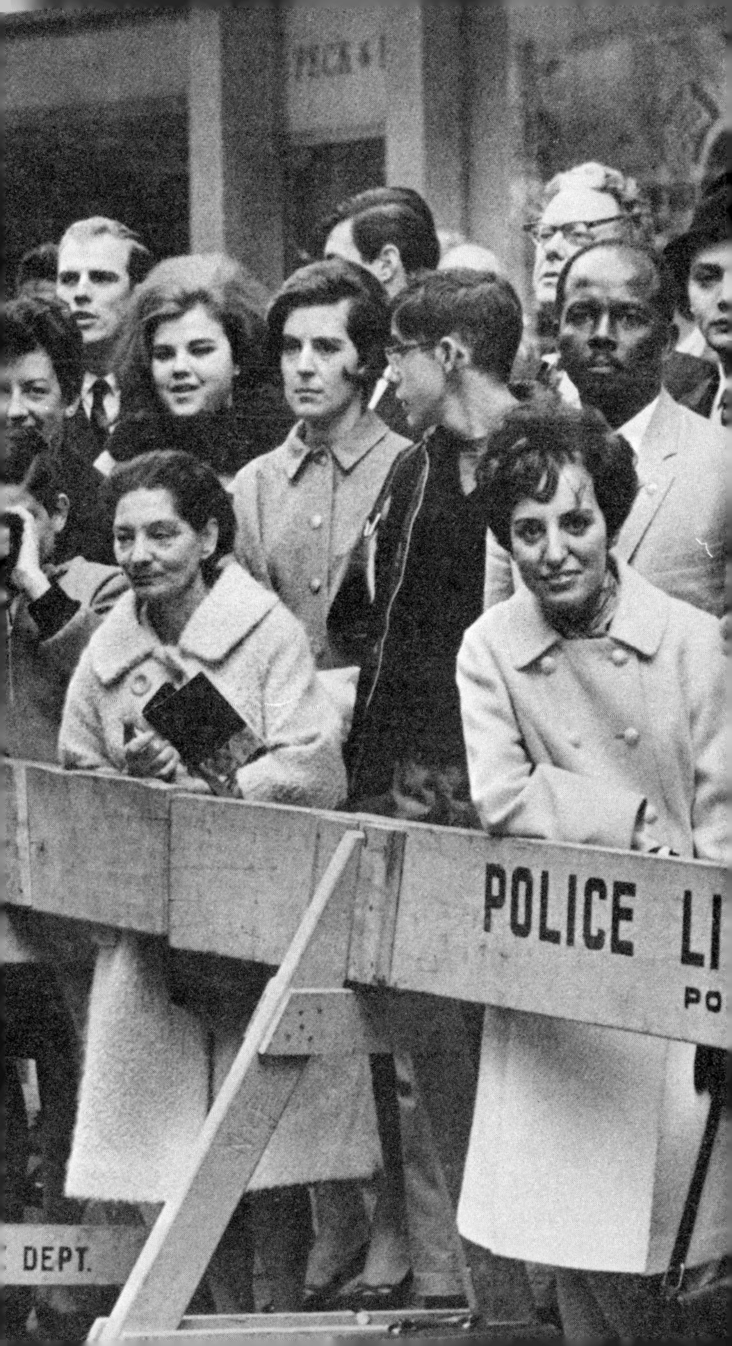
POLICE LI
PO
DEPT.

Conversation

People's speech varies as much as their appearance and personality. The phrases people choose, and the accent with which they pronounce them, depend on the place they come from, their education and their age, as well as personality. A person's speech is often as good a "clue" as his appearance.

Writing natural-sounding dialogue is not as easy as you might think. It requires very careful *listening*, first of all, to catch the expressions people use to express emotions or just to pass the time of day. This is how Dr. Eric Berne, author of *Games People Play*, reproduces what he calls the "American greeting ritual."

"Hi!" (Hello, good morning)
"Hi!" (Hello, good morning)
"Warm enough forya?" (How are you?)
"Sure is. Looks like rain, though." (Fine. How are you?)
"Well, take cara yourself." (Okay)
"I'll be seeing you."
"So long."
"So long."

—Eric Berne, *Games People Play*

Exercise 48:

Does that sound like the "greeting ritual" in your part of the country? Listen carefully to the next greeting you hear exchanged on the street, in the school corridor, or on the phone. Jot the phrases down on a scrap of paper, if you can. Write two different "greeting rituals" of about eight exchanges each (as above)—one exchanged by your own friends, and the other exchanged by your parents, teachers or older people. How do they differ? Reproduce the slang, and the sound of the words ("forya") as exactly as you can.

Keeping a notebook to catch the sounds of real speech is an excellent idea, practiced by many writers. Buy a notebook at the dime store, small enough to fit into your pocket or purse. Every day, write down a few snatches of conversation, or unusual phrases you have overheard. Some professionals fill notebook after notebook with such talk, as well as observations and ideas for stories. Later, you can work your scribbled notes into the conversations of many stories and plays.

Exercise 49:

Imagine what is happening in this photo—a basketball game? A music group? Look at the emotions on the girls' faces. Try to write half a page reproducing typical sounds that they (and the boys behind them) are making during the game or show. Don't confine yourself to complete sentences, or even to real words. Be as imaginative as you can in reproducing the sounds of shrieks, yells, screams, boos, laughs, cheers and crying. Be as realistic as possible.

The "spoken" phrases you write must sound natural. Read them aloud to yourself, several times. Do they ring true? They must be right for the time and place in your story, and for the character of the speaker. If your speaker lives in the rural South, his phrases and accent will not sound like those spoken in Brooklyn. Contrasts between your various characters should show up in their speech—an extreme example would be a boy from Mississippi talking to an old lady from London, England. And if you are writing about today, you wouldn't dream of using slang from years ago, like "Hotcha!" or "Twenty-three Skidoo!" or "Gee Whillikers!" (If you want to see good examples of outmoded slang, read the stories by O. Henry. He had a sharp ear for the speech of his time and place—New York around 1900.)

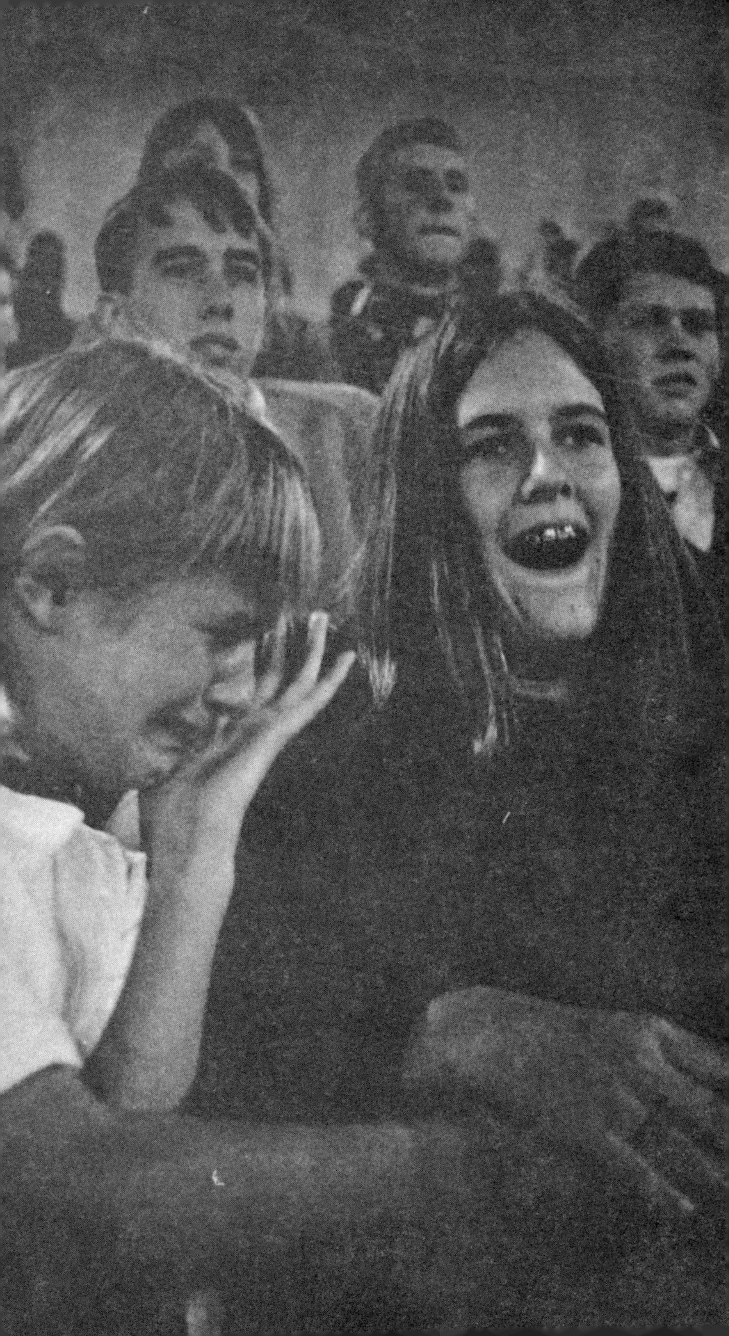

A pitfall in writing conversation is the temptation of saying too much. Real talk often has an abrupt, staccato quality. It is also easy to forget that, in real life, one speaker does not always listen to what the other is saying. People interrupt each other, misunderstand, or ramble off on digressions. Natural conversations do not necessarily go in a straight line.

Exercise 50:

Imagine you are with these two boys and the girl. Try to write a page of natural conversation that is taking place along with the guitar music and singing. The conversation can be aimless, and there can be gaps of silence, while music is played. Just reproduce casual remarks, questions or jokes, spoken at times during that afternoon. Use slang, if you like, and make it sound like real talk.

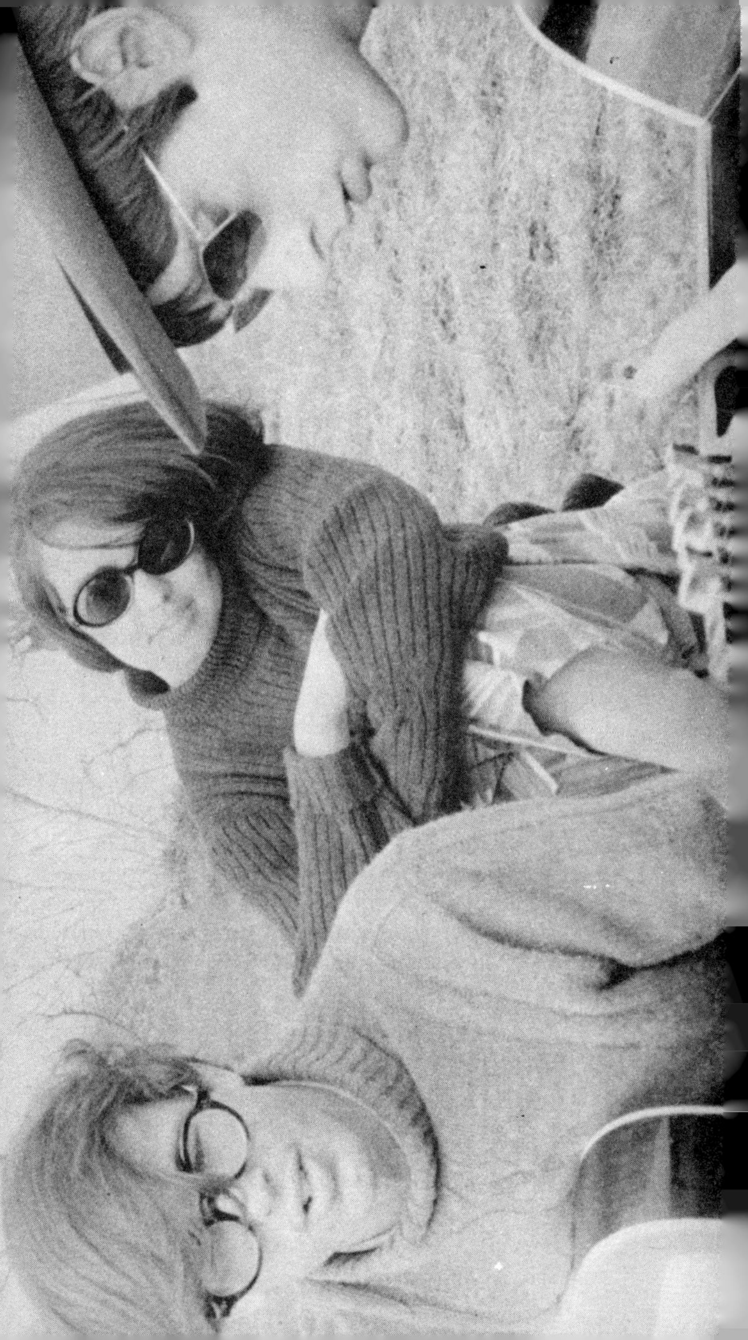

When people get emotional—excited, angry or frightened—their speech changes just as much as their facial expressions. A good writer can use speech to *show* the emotions his characters are feeling, instead of just *telling* the reader about them. In many of the best novels and stories, the person of the author never intrudes between the reader and the fictional characters. The reader is able to draw his own conclusions, without any helpful promptings from the author. In stage plays, of course, the author is not "present" and is unable to give any running commentary, so the characters' words and actions have to speak for themselves.

Exercise 51:

Has the teacher told the boy to stay after class to be scolded for misbehavior? Or has the boy come to her to ask for help? Is he in trouble? Is the teacher angry or sympathetic? Think out an imaginary situation. Then write half a page (or more) of dialogue between the teacher and the student. Make their emotions unmistakably clear. Make their talk sound realistic.

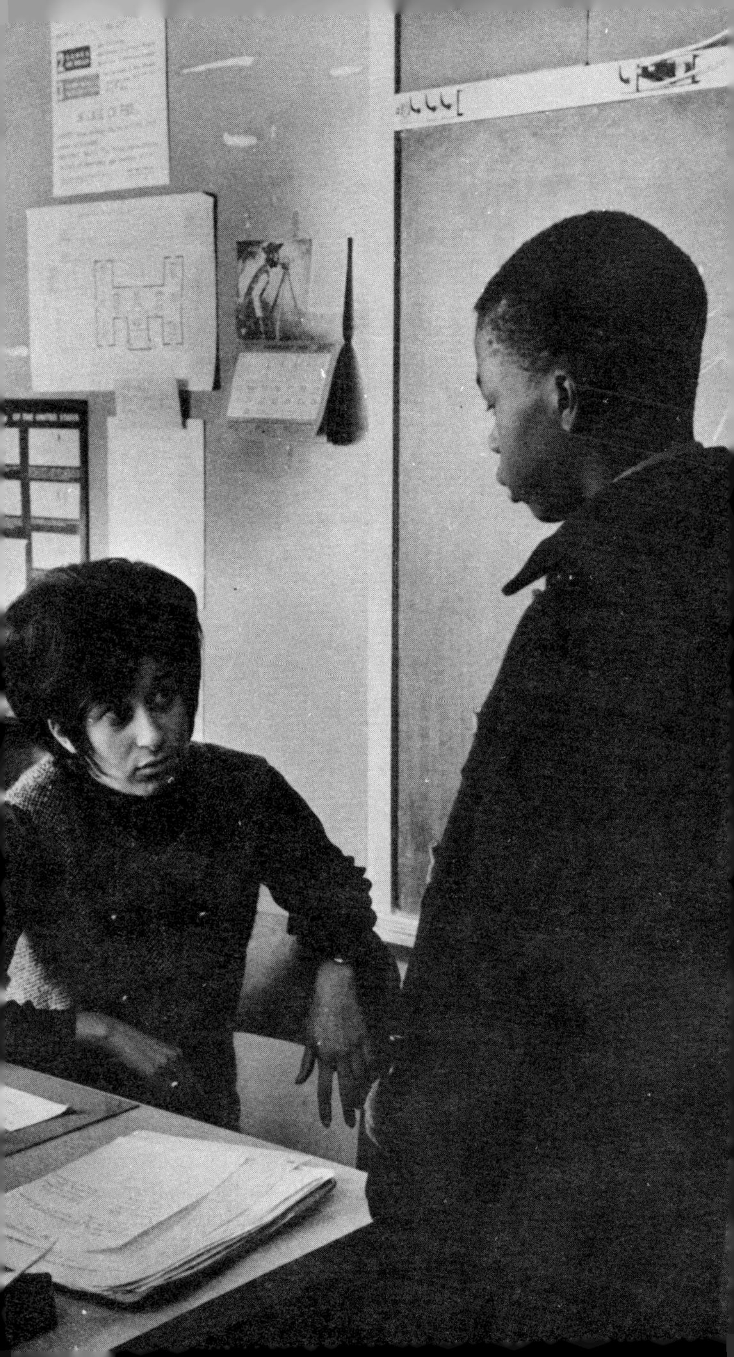

Exercise 52:

This boy is arguing about the war in Vietnam, at a booth set up by protestors. He may be disagreeing with the person running the booth. Or he may agree with the protest and be arguing with another bystander who supports the war. In either case, he is excited, aggressive and a bit angry. Decide on his position about the war. Then write half a page (or more) of the impromptu "speech" he is making. Show his emotions. Make his language sound real.

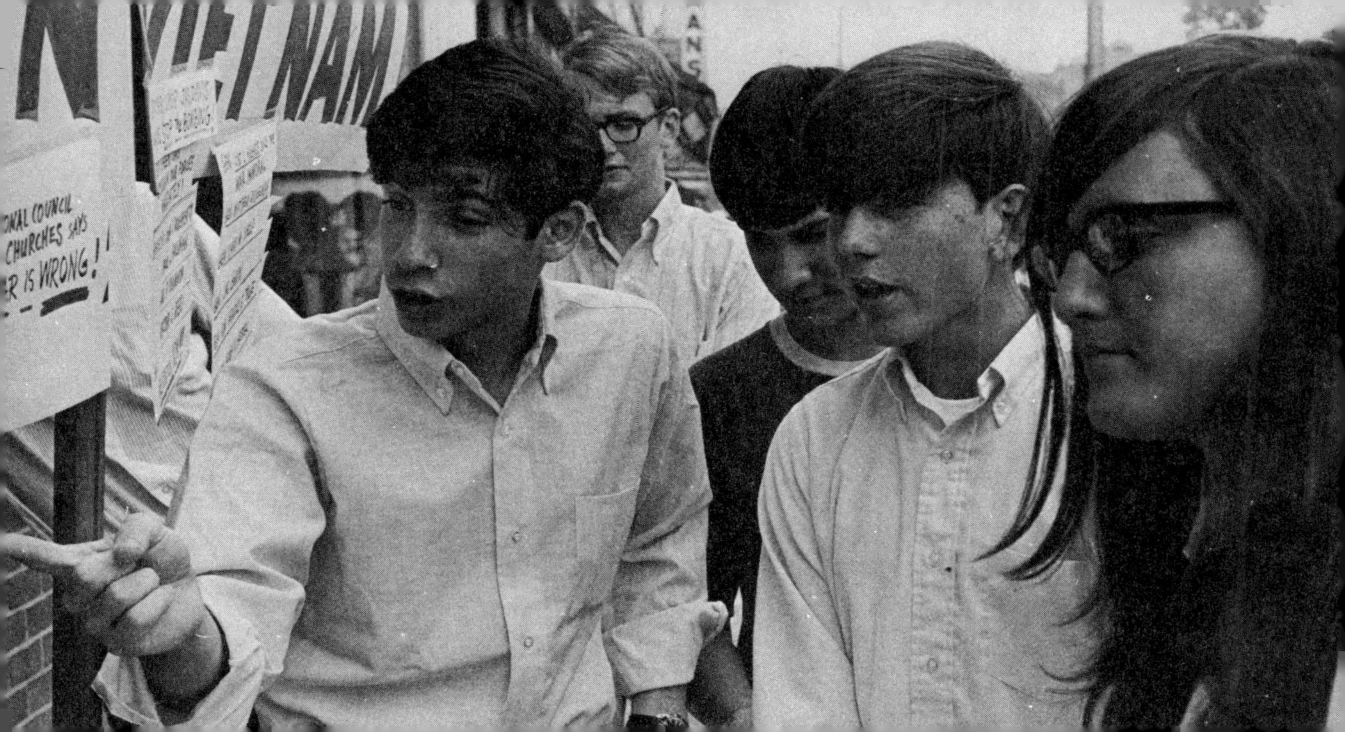
VIETNAM
ONAL COUNCIL
CHURCHES SAYS
ER IS WRONG!

132

Exercise 53:

Look at the two men. Write half a page or more of realistic conversation between them. Show their characters, and the effects of the liquor. Try to make their conversation the start of a story, in which some action is taken by the men.

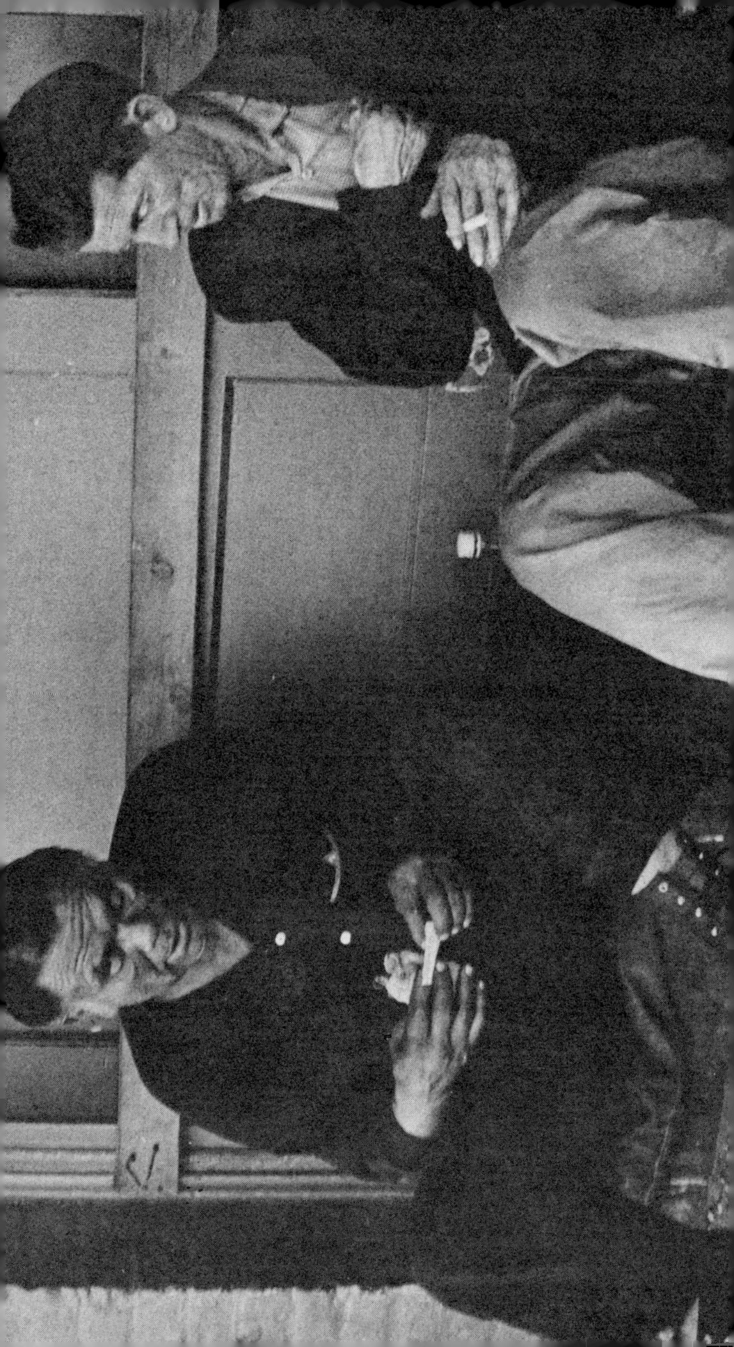

People often talk about other people. People love to gossip, even when their talk is not meant to be unkind. Such talk is very relaxed. As they gossip, the talkers sometimes reveal as much about themselves as about the subject of their conversation. Are they jealous? Admiring? Competitive? Sarcastic? Here is the beginning of some gossip, from Eudora Welty's "Petrified Man," a story told entirely in dialogue.

"Reach in my purse and git me a cigarette without no powder on it if you kin, Mrs. Fletcher, honey," said Leota to her ten o'clock shampoo-and-set customer. "I don't like no perfumed cigarettes."

Mrs. Fletcher gladly reached over to the lavender shelf under the lavender-framed mirror, shook a hair net loose from the clasp of the patent-leather bag, and slapped her hand down quickly on a powder puff which burst out when the purse was opened.

"Why, look at the peanuts, Leota!" said Mrs. Fletcher in her marveling voice.

"Honey, them goobers has been in my purse a week if they's been in it a day. Mrs. Pike bought them peanuts."

"Who's Mrs. Pike?" asked Mrs. Fletcher, settling back. Hidden in this den of curling fluid and henna packs, separated by a lavender swing door from the other customers, who were being gratified in other booths, she could give her curiosity its freedom. She looked expectantly at the black part in Leota's yellow curls as she bent to light the cigarette.

"Mrs. Pike is this lady from New Orleans," said Leota, puffing, and pressing into Mrs. Fletcher's scalp with strong red-nailed fingers. "A friend, not a customer. You see, like maybe I told you last time, me and Fred and Sal and Joe all had us a fuss, so Sal and Joe up and moved out, so we didn't do a thing but rent out their room. So we rented it to Mrs. Pike. And Mr. Pike." She flicked an ash into the basket of dirty towels. "Mrs. Pike is a very decided blonde. *She* bought me the peanuts."

"She must be cute," said Mrs. Fletcher.

"Honey, 'cute' ain't the word for what she is. I'm tellin' you, Mrs. Pike is attractive. She has her 'a good time. She's got a sharp eye out, Mrs. Pike has."

She dashed the comb through the air, and paused dramatically....
—Eudora Welty, "Petrified Man"
(From *A Curtain of Green*)

Exercise 54:

Compare the next two pictures. The two pairs of talkers are very different, and their styles of speech will not be the same. Choose one of the two couples. Pretend they are gossiping about a third person. Write one page of their relaxed conversation, making the talk realistic. Make the speakers reveal something of their own personality, as well as the character of their subject. Now and then, add brief passages about their gestures or expressions, and give some references to their surroundings.

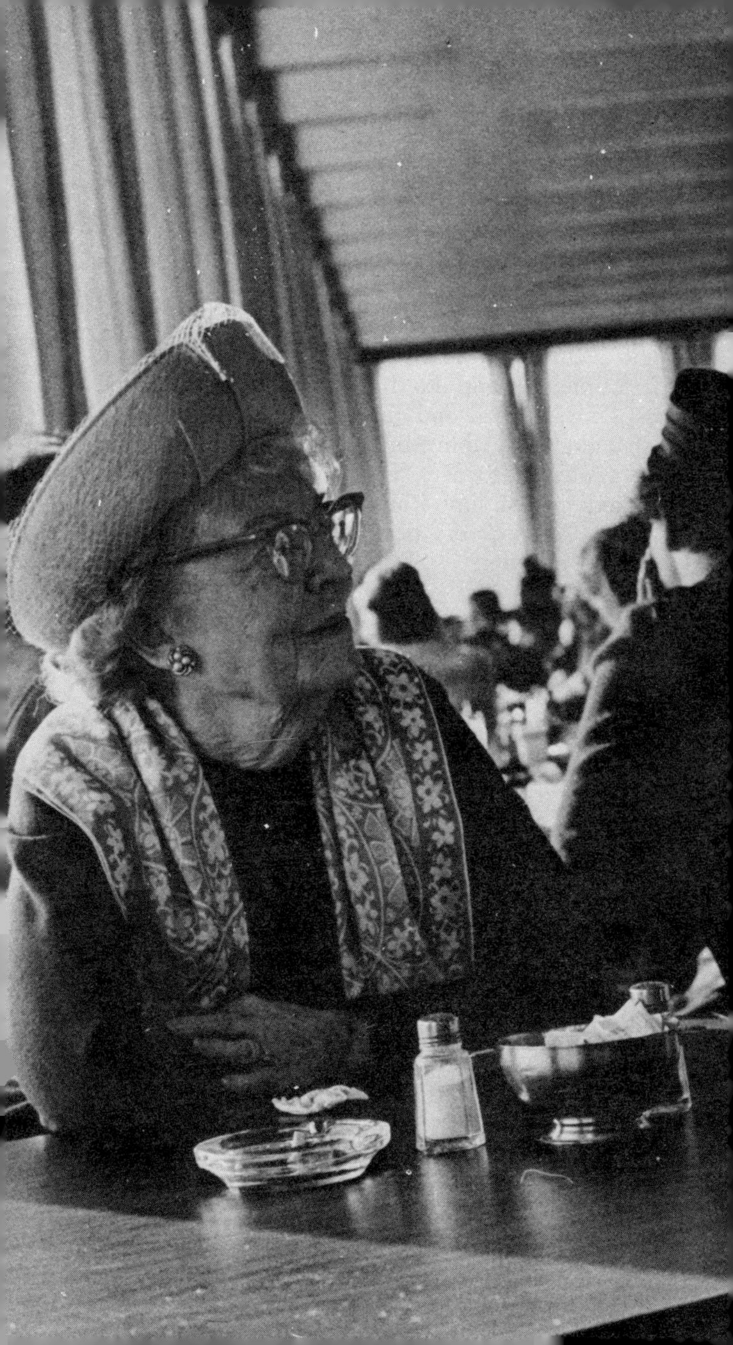

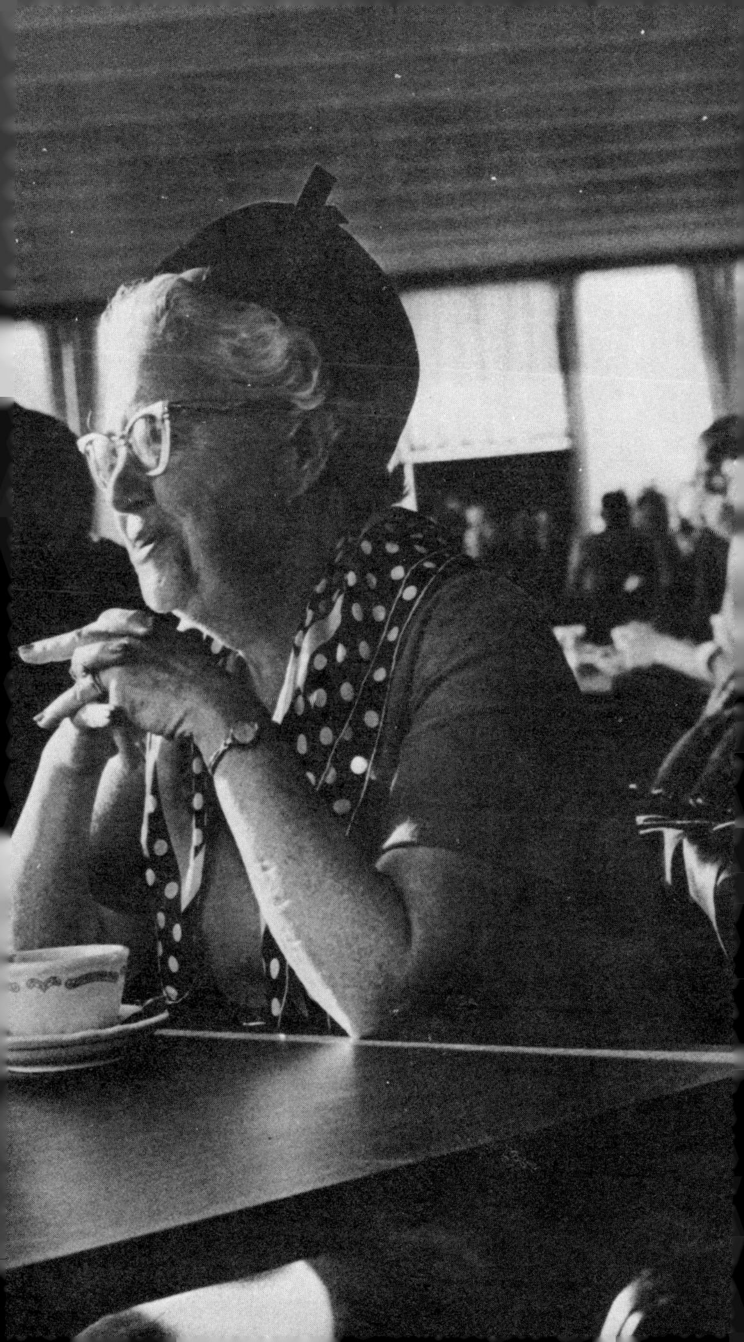

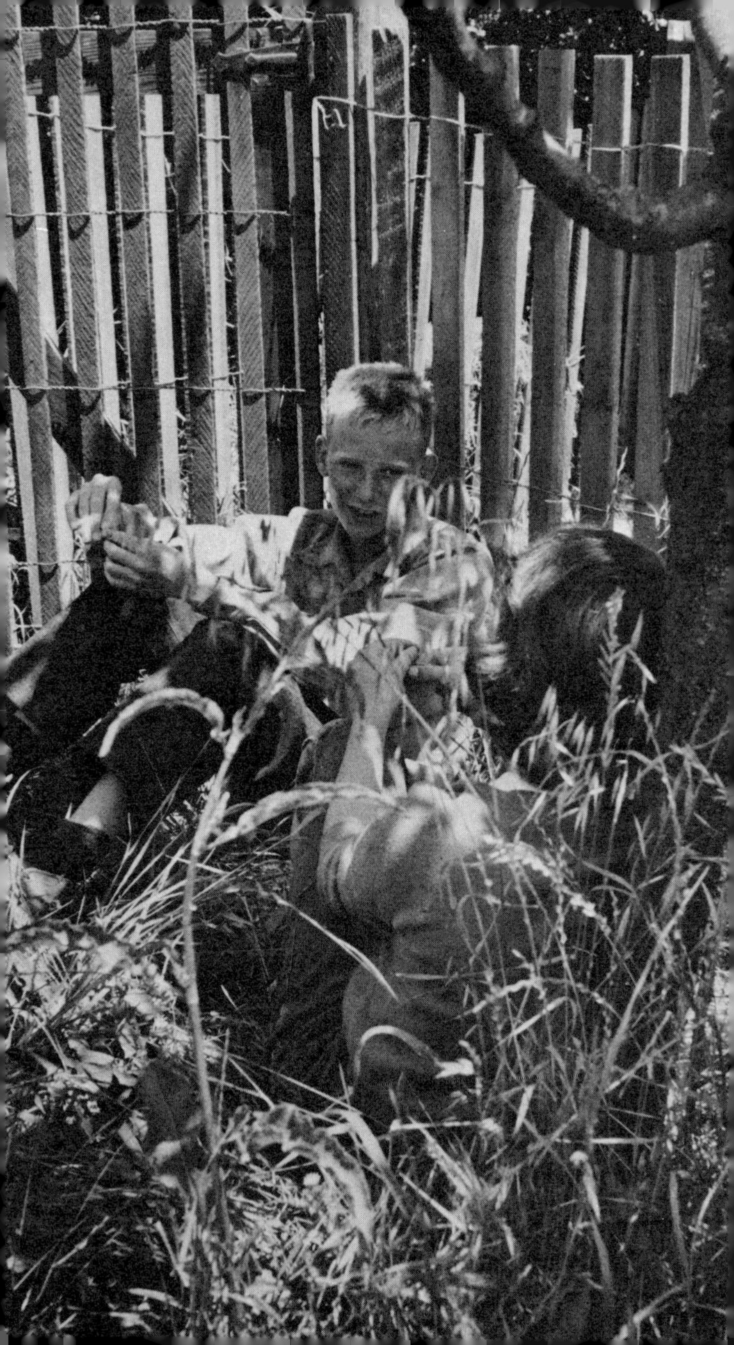

Plot
Dramatic
Tension

What holds a reader's interest? Descriptions, characters and conversations are quite interesting in themselves. But they are not usually enough to make a reader feel that he simply can't put a book down. As a reader yourself, think of the last time you had that feeling. Why did you *have* to get to the end of the book? Probably, it was to learn how the plot came out—what happened to the characters?

The plot's dramatic tension was what held you riveted to the pages. Drama is the key element in the longest novels, plays, and the shortest short stories. Without the dramatic interest of a problem that must be solved by the main character, or a conflict between him and some opposing person or force, any writing will be dull and lifeless.

Conflict is what causes tension—literally, "the state of being stretched or strained" in two opposite directions. The strain causes interest and excitement. Which side is going to snap first? In most plots, conflict follows the same general pattern: a character conceives a purpose, and another character (or impersonal force) opposes him, trying to prevent him from succeeding. The conflict may be between man and man, or man and fate, or both.

For example, one of the oldest plots in the world is the love story: boy meets girl, boy loses girl, boy wins girl back again. The real drama begins at the end of stage two, as the boy faces the problems of winning back his girl. The conflict may be between him and a rival, between him and the fate that puts him at some disadvantage, or simply between him and a girl who can't make up her mind. In any case, tension mounts until the conflict is resolved, one way or another.

The hero, of course, does not always win. As playwright Bernard Shaw wrote, "The end may be reconciliation or destruction; or, as in life, there may be no end; but the conflict is indispensable: no conflict, no drama."

A plot may have many different conflicts, at once or one after the other. In a mystery story, problem after problem crops up, until you begin to wonder whether the criminal will ever be caught.

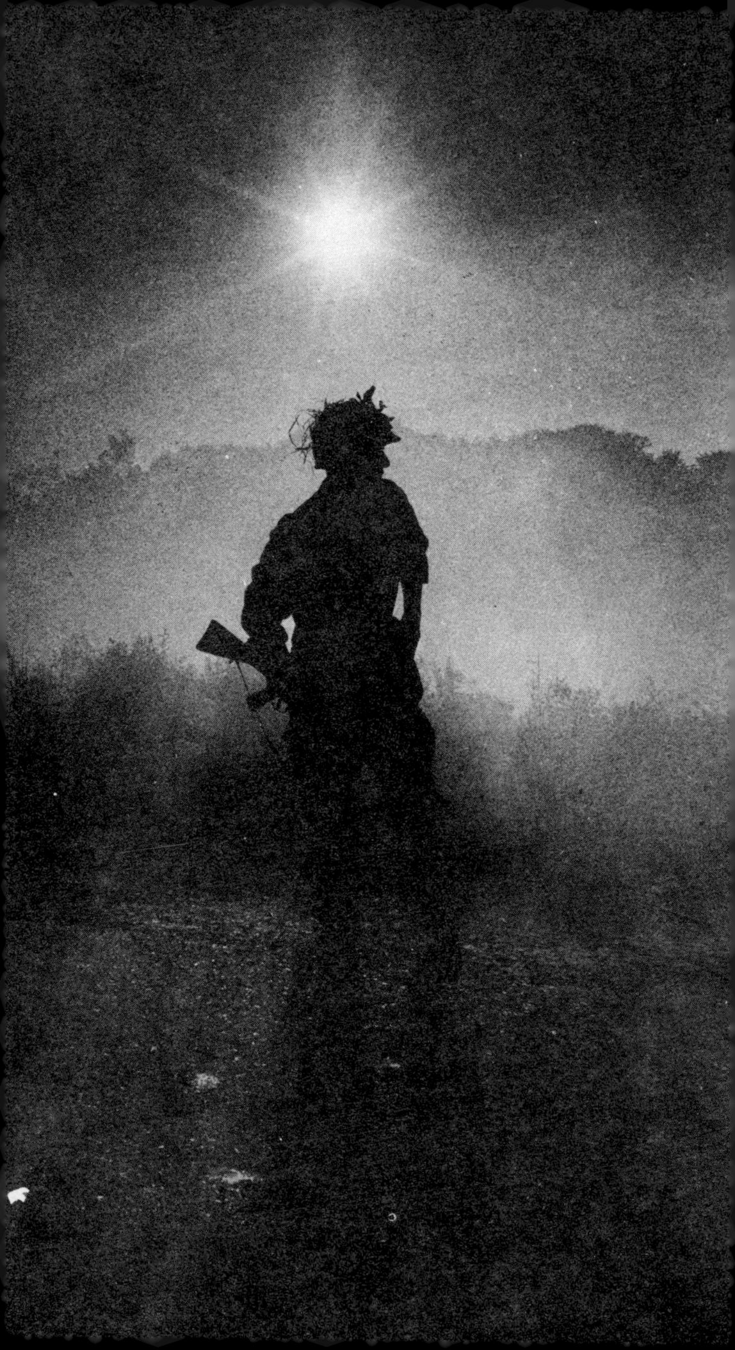

Exercise 55:

Small details, like the ticking of a clock, are often used to build up the suspense of a tense scene. Look carefully at the soldier on the misty road. All his senses are alert, prepared for possible conflict. Describe this scene, setting a mood that is very tense. What is the soldier looking at? What does he hear, apart from his own boots on the gravel? Use techniques you learned in the chapters on senses and on scene and mood to make your reader feel the suspense, the suppressed excitement.

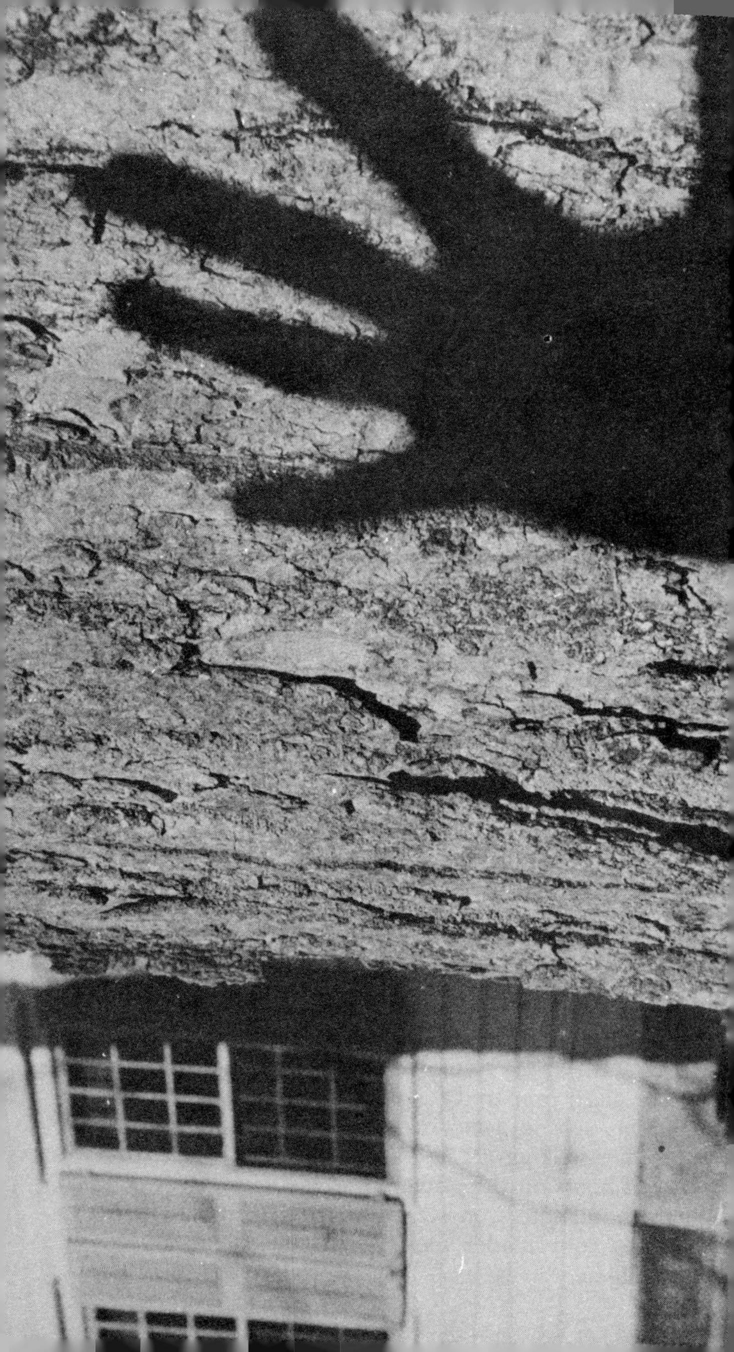

Exercise 56:

Use your imagination to create a mood of suspense based on this picture. Your writing might be part of a story about spies, murder or ghosts. Is the light and shadow caused by sun or moonlight? To whom does the upraised hand belong? Are the people inside the house aware of his presence? What is about to happen next? Use sensory details to make your writing as exciting and threatening as possible. Bring the reader up to the moment of conflict.

Exercise 57:

The next picture shows the actual moment of conflict of the most dramatic sort. The fans of bull fighting regard it as drama, as well as an athletic sport. Using techniques you practiced in the chapter on point of view, put yourself in the matador's place. Describe the contest between yourself and the bull. Make it as exciting and active as possible. Use sensory details about the bull, the heat and dust, the sounds of the crowd. Describe your own emotions.

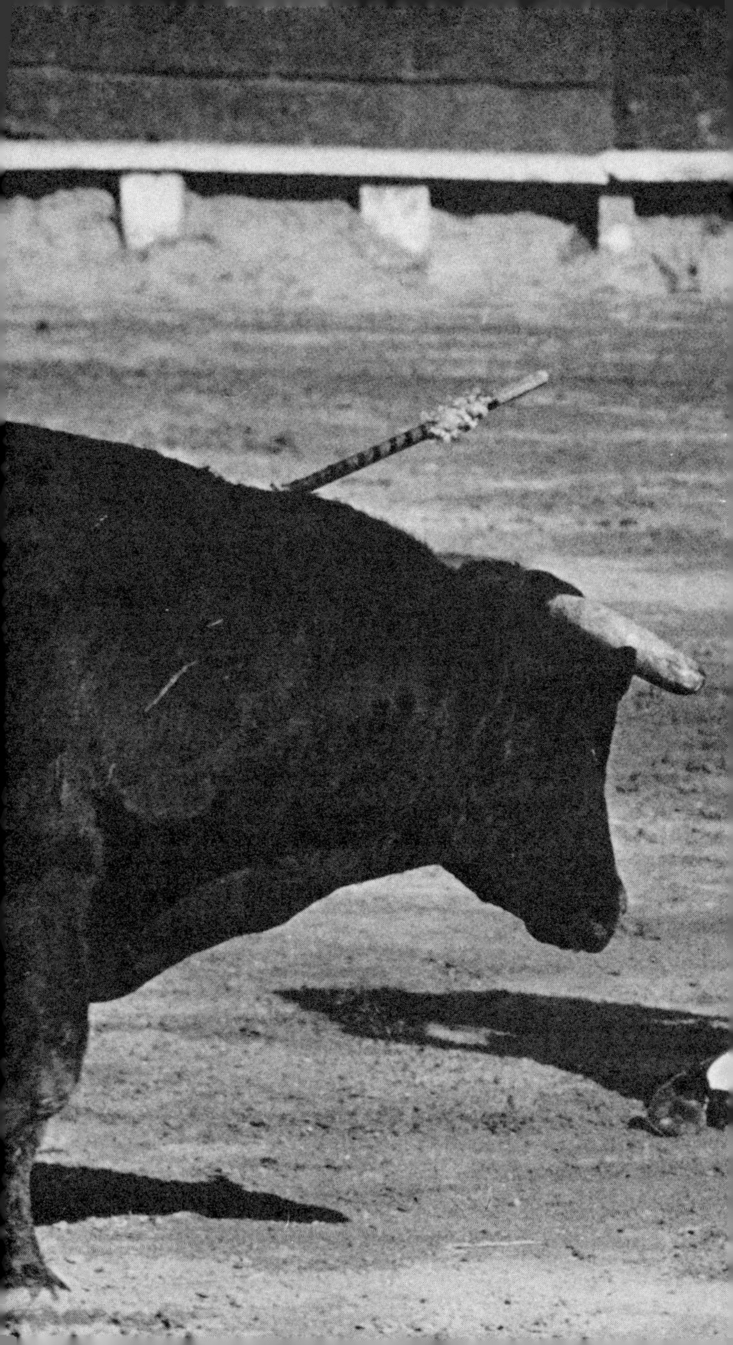

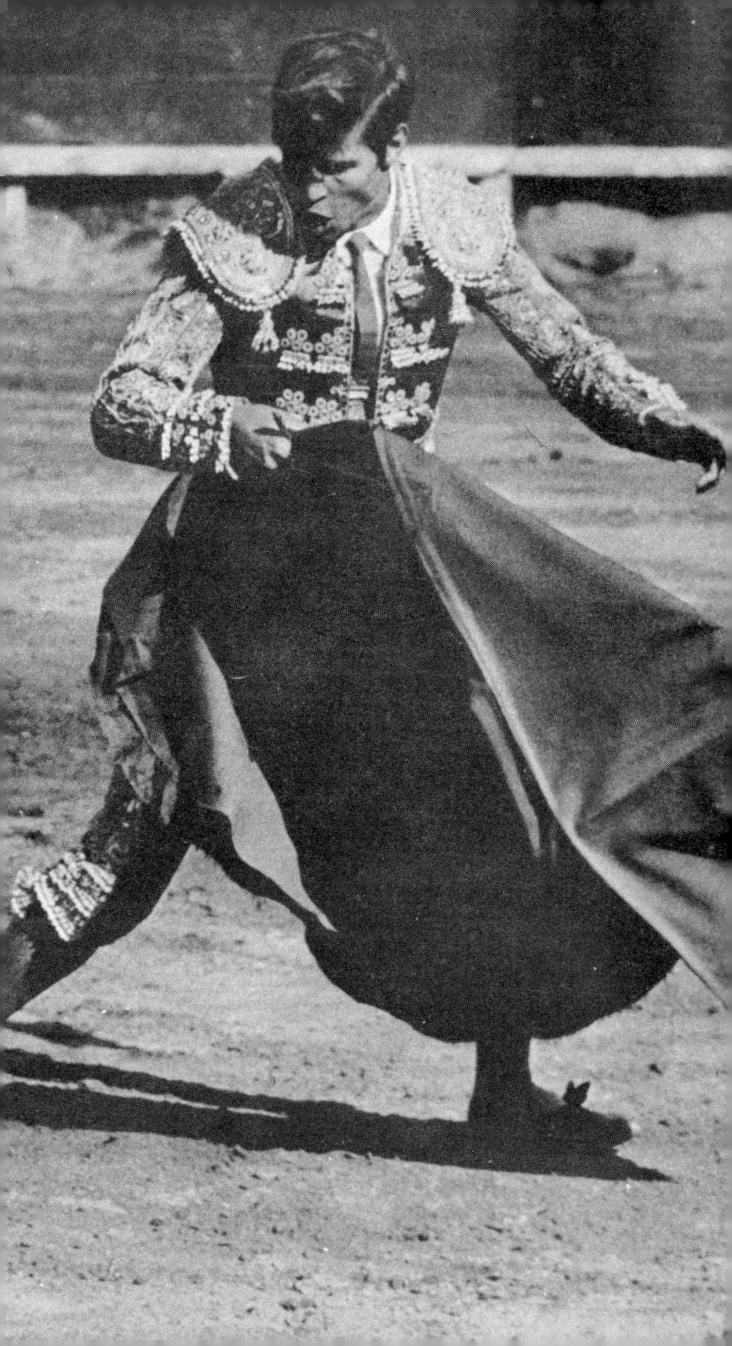

Exercise 58:

The moment of physical conflict has just ended, in this picture. The photo is perhaps the most dramatic ever taken of the war in Vietnam. The drama lies largely in the central appeal for help—the soldier with arms raised is signaling to a rescue helicopter. Others help the wounded. The "conflict" now is between the soldiers and disaster. Using what you learned in the chapter on point of view, describe the scene through the eyes of one of the soldiers—perhaps the one waving, or the wounded one in the foreground. Include facial expressions and snatches of talk (practiced in the sections on people and conversation). Include sensory details.

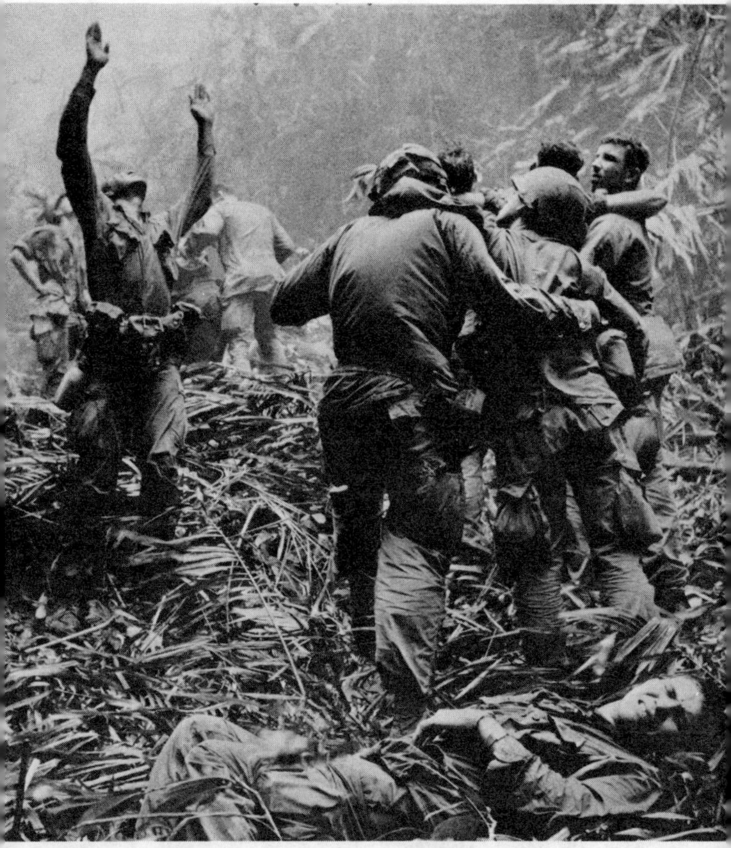

Exercise 59:

Something dramatic has just happened in this picture. A crowd has gathered to watch the ensuing conflict. The conflict is verbal and emotional, not really physical. Shouts of accusation and insult are being exchanged. Pretend that you are in the crowd. Using the techniques you learned in the chapters on people and conversation, describe the people you are watching. Reproduce some of their shouts. What do you think has just happened to cause this? Make the conflict as sharp as possible. Carry the conflict to its resolution—someone giving up and walking away, or the arrival of the police, perhaps.

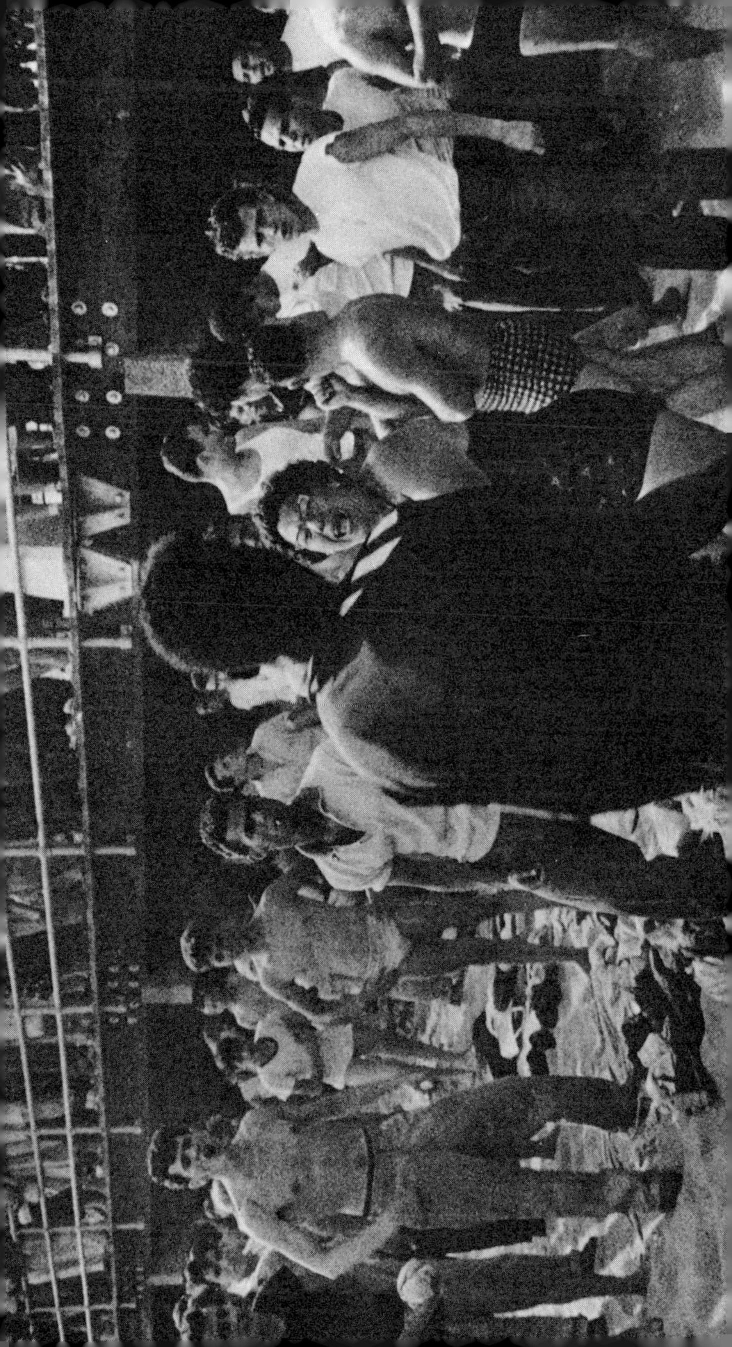

Exercise 60:

The pictures on the next two pages show two kinds of physical conflict. One is a direct fight. The second is a competition between several people, only one of whom can win the race. Choose one of the two pictures. Write a complete short story, with a plot that centers on this conflict.

If you choose the picture on page 153, introduce the three young men—their appearance and personalities—in an opening scene. Give an account of the events leading up to the fight, including snatches of realistic talk. Did the victim deserve to be attacked, two-to-one? Was it a surprise attack? Build up the tension before hand, then describe the actual fight and its final resolution.

If you choose the other picture, introduce the competitors, and the surroundings in which they will race. Take the viewpoint of one of the runners, if you like. Then describe the race, with as many exciting details as you can, building up to the climax at the finish line.

In either story, who wins? Are your sympathies with the winner? Without writing any actual "moral" at the end, try to give your story some unspoken, underlying point or meaning.

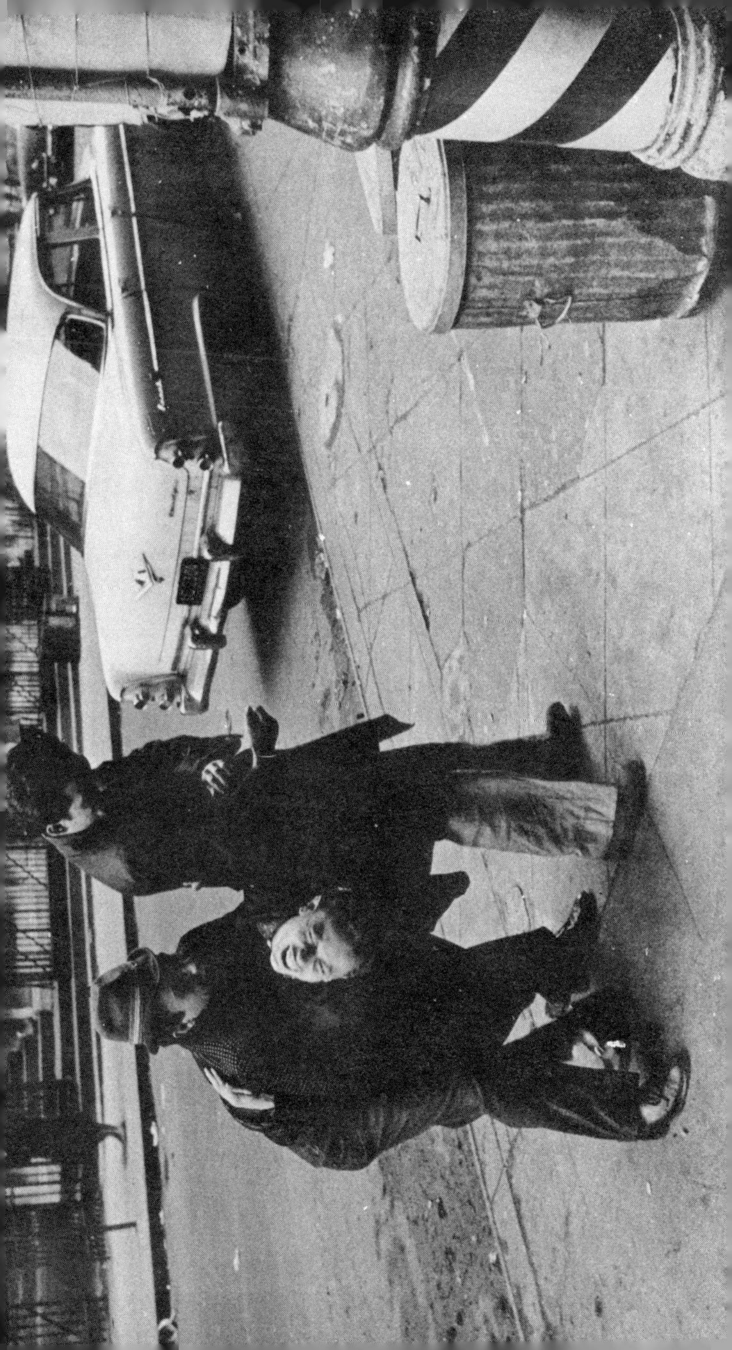

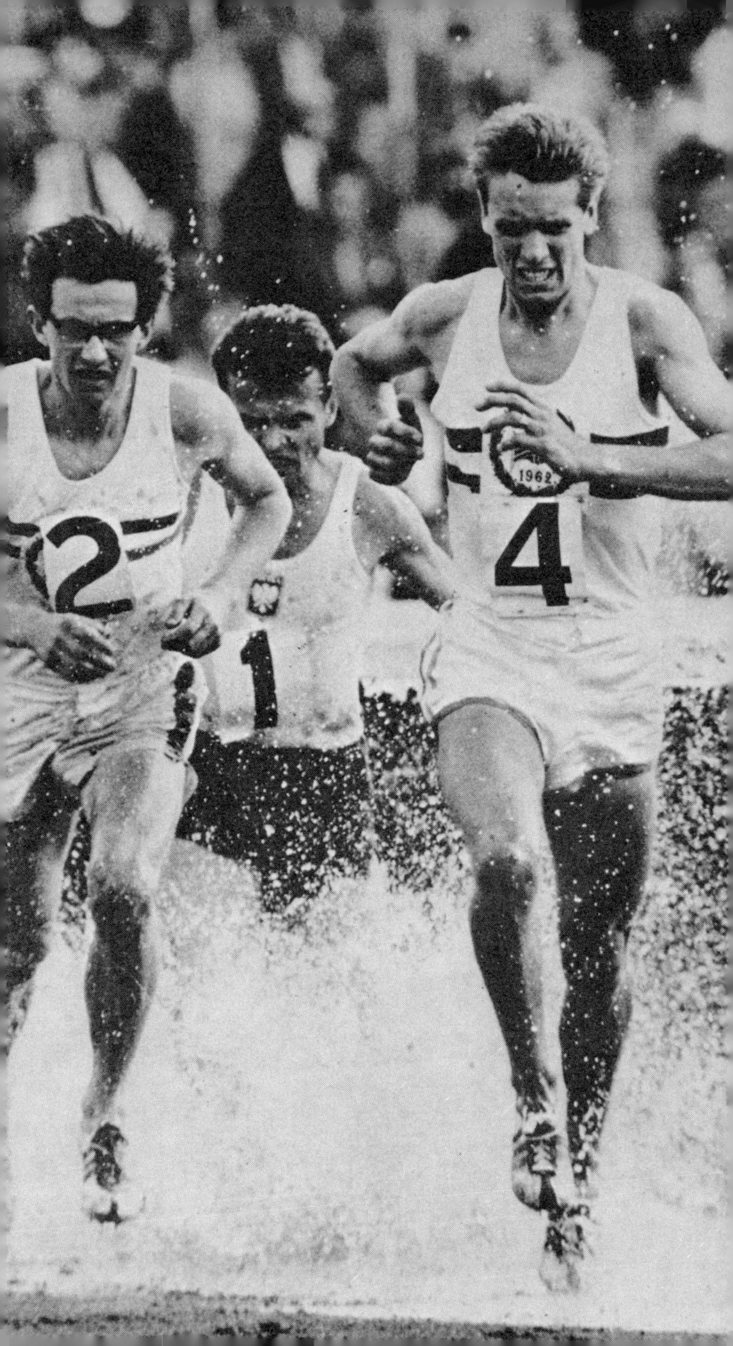
2
1
1962
4

Surprise
And
Comedy

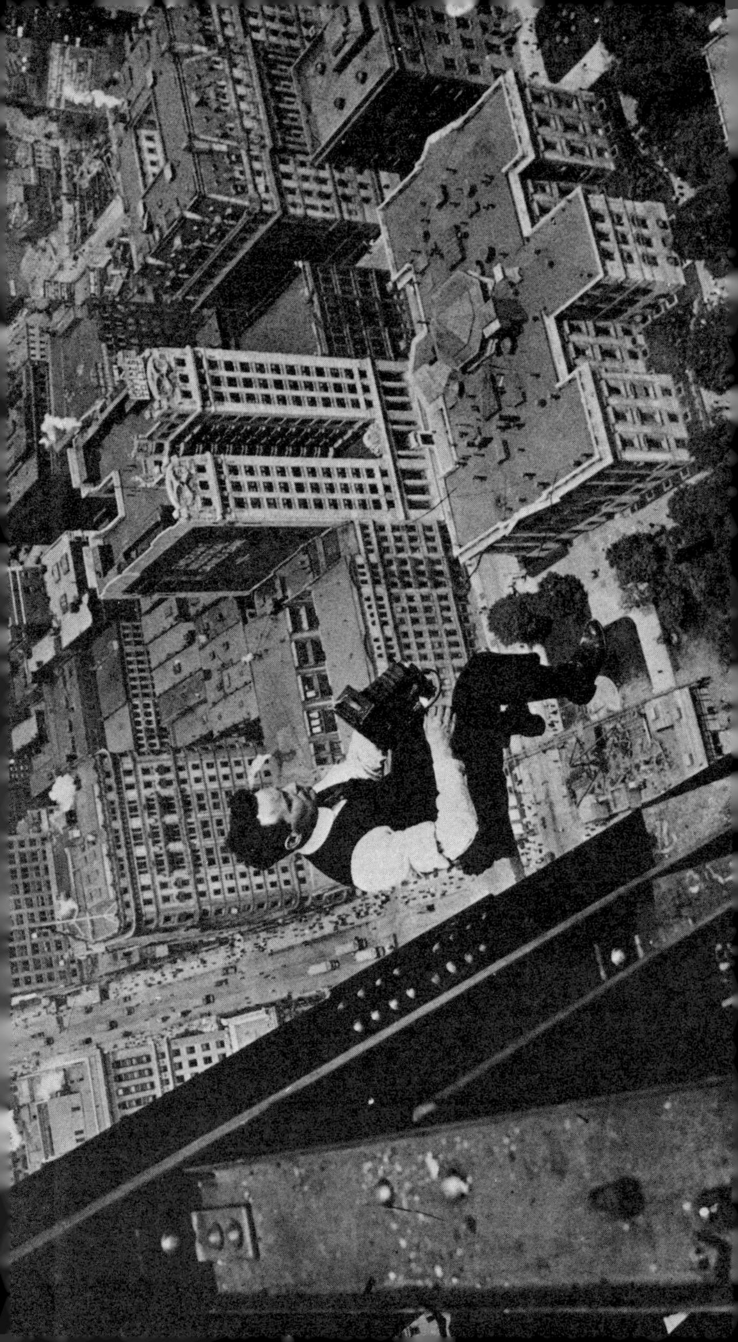

Surprise can be a very effective way of increasing the drama of your plot. But it is a challenging technique to try, because in the hands of an unskillful writer it runs the danger of looking like a cheap trick, played on the reader. The stunning effect of a successful surprise is worth trying. It should be an honest surprise, completely unexpected, consistent with the plot, but making the reader feel almost as if someone had punched him in the stomach.

Do you get that feeling as you look at the daredevil photographer of 1912, perched in sickening space beside the high girders of the Woolworth Building? Words can shock as strongly as that visual surprise. Here is the climax from Edgar Allan Poe's "The Fall of the House of Usher"—Madeline's return from the coffin, in which her brother buried her alive:

... the huge antique panels to which the speaker pointed drew slowly back, upon the instant, their ponderous and ebony jaws. It was the work of the rushing gust—but then without the doors there *did* stand the lofty and enshrouded figure of the lady Madeline of Usher. There was blood upon her white robes, and the evidence of some bitter struggle upon every portion of her emaciated frame. For a moment she remained trembling and reeling to and fro upon the threshold—then, with a low moaning cry, fell heavily inward upon the person of her brother, and, in her violent and now final death agonies, bore him to the floor a corpse, and a victim to the terrors he had anticipated.
—Edgar Allan Poe, "The Fall of the House of Usher"

Surprise endings can be hard to write convincingly. Worn-out endings, like a story of incredible adventures that turns out to have been a dream, cheat the reader. Try thinking up a surprise ending to some of the stories you have been planning and writing so far.

The whole point of Guy de Maupassant's story, "The Necklace", lies in its surprise ending. It took a master storyteller to carry this off successfully. He tells the story of a middle-class French couple, a hundred years ago. It is the story of an extraordinarily beautiful diamond necklace, borrowed from a friend and then lost by the vain, foolish wife. Buying a duplicate, and returning it without a word, they change their whole lives—moving to a garret, slaving from dawn to dark for ten years. Finally, their debt is paid off.

Madame Loisel looked old now. She had become like all the other strong, hard, coarse women of poor households. Her hair was badly done, her skirts were awry, her hands were red. She spoke in a shrill voice, and the water slopped all over the floor when she scrubbed it. But sometimes, when her husband was at the office, she sat down by the window and thought of that evening long ago, of the ball at which she had been so beautiful and so much admired.

What would have happened if she had never lost the jewels? Who knows? Who knows? How strange life is, how fickle! How little is needed to ruin or save!

One Sunday, as she had gone for a walk along the Champs-Elysées to freshen herself after the labours of the week, she caught sight suddenly of a woman who was taking a child out for a walk. It was Madame Forestier, still young, still beautiful, still attractive.

Madame Loisel was conscious of some emotion. Should she speak to her? Yes, certainly. And now that she had paid, she would tell her all. Why not?

She went up to her. "Good morning, Jeanne."

The other did not recognise her, and was surprised at being thus familiarly addressed by a poor woman. "But...madame..." she stammered. "I don't know...you must be making a mistake."

"No...I am Mathilde Loisel."

Her friend uttered a cry. "Oh!...my poor Mathilde, how you have changed!..."

"Yes, I've had some hard times since I saw you last, and many sorrows...and all on your account."

"On my account!...How was that?"

"You remember the diamond necklace you lent me for the ball at the Ministry?"

"Yes. Well?"

"Well, I lost it."

"How could you? Why, you brought it back."

"I brought you another just like it. And for the last ten years we have been paying for it. You realise it wasn't easy for us; we had no money... Well, it's paid for at last, and I'm mighty glad."

Madame Forestier had halted. "You say you bought a diamond necklace to replace mine?"

"Yes. You hadn't noticed it? They were very much alike." And she smiled in proud and innocent happiness.

Madame Forestier, deeply moved, took her two hands.

"Oh, my poor Mathilde! But mine was imitation. It was worth at the very most only five hundred francs!..."   —Guy de Maupassant, "The Necklace"

Surprise is often funny. In fact, surprise is probably the essence of humor. Humorous writing comes easily to some writers, almost like a natural gift, but most writers find it takes a lot of practice, a lot of trial and error. *Timing* is the secret of a good stage comedian, who can make the whole audience laugh at his jokes. As you try to describe funny scenes and incidents, pay careful attention to the timing of your writing—how quickly should you pass on to the next detail? Are you slowly building up to a good "punch line"? Or are you keeping your readers in a steady state of amusement, with one funny detail after another?

Exercise 61:

Why do you find this picture surprising? What is funny? The key to the picture's impact is the missing head. You expected to see a head on the figure. Instead, the white neck sticks foolishly up into space. The unexpected absense of something can be funny in many different ways. Try to think of a joke in which the punch line is the absence of something expected. Write the joke down. Read it aloud to yourself. Get the "timing" of the phrases right, and word it so that you think it sounds really funny. If you can't think of a joke about something missing, write down any other joke that amuses you.

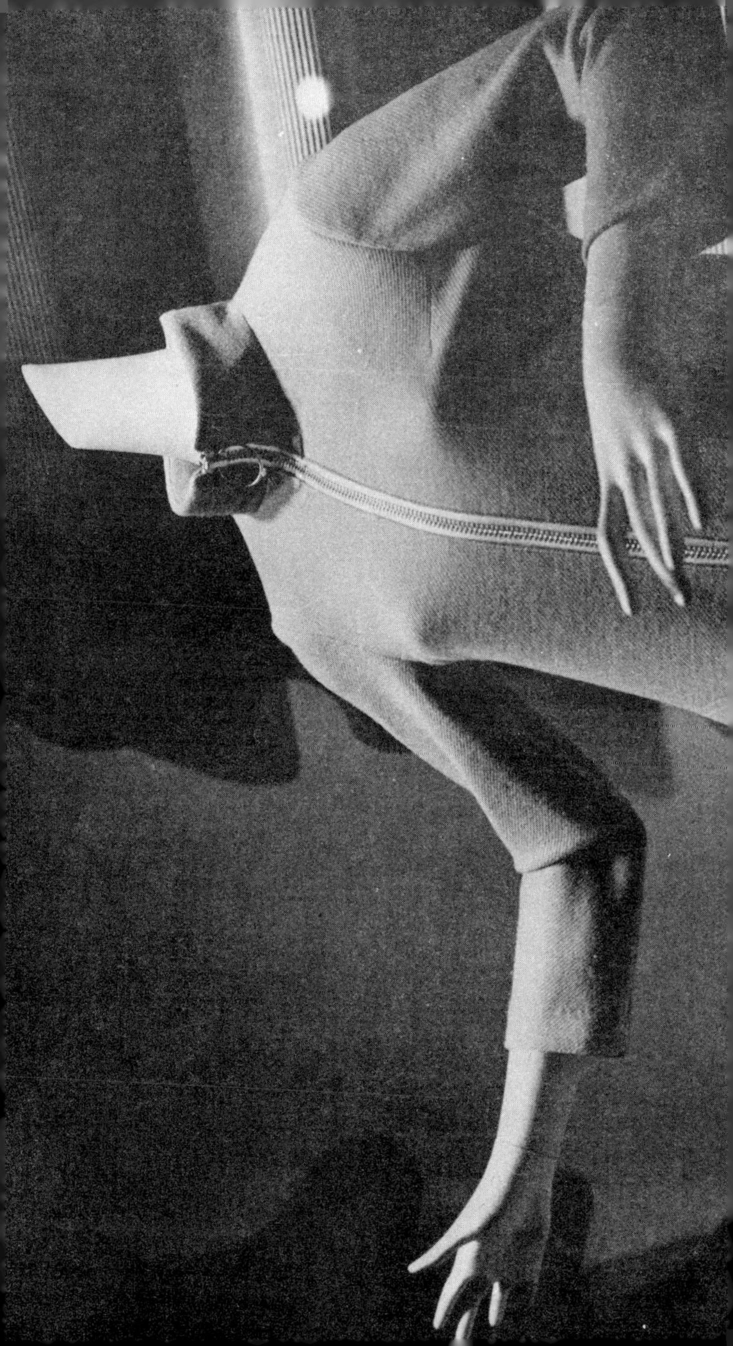

Exercise 62:

Why is this picture so funny? It is largely the opposite of the humor in the last picture. Instead of unexpected absence, here is unexpected presence. Here is the presence of something you never expected to see—a kitten in the spaghetti pot. Another funny aspect is the silly grin on the kitten's own face, as if it, too, found the thing amusing. You probably laughed, also, because for a moment you imagined the expression on the cook's face. As if you were sitting in the kitchen, describe the scene in the picture. Include the cook's reactions, if you like. Make it as funny as you can.

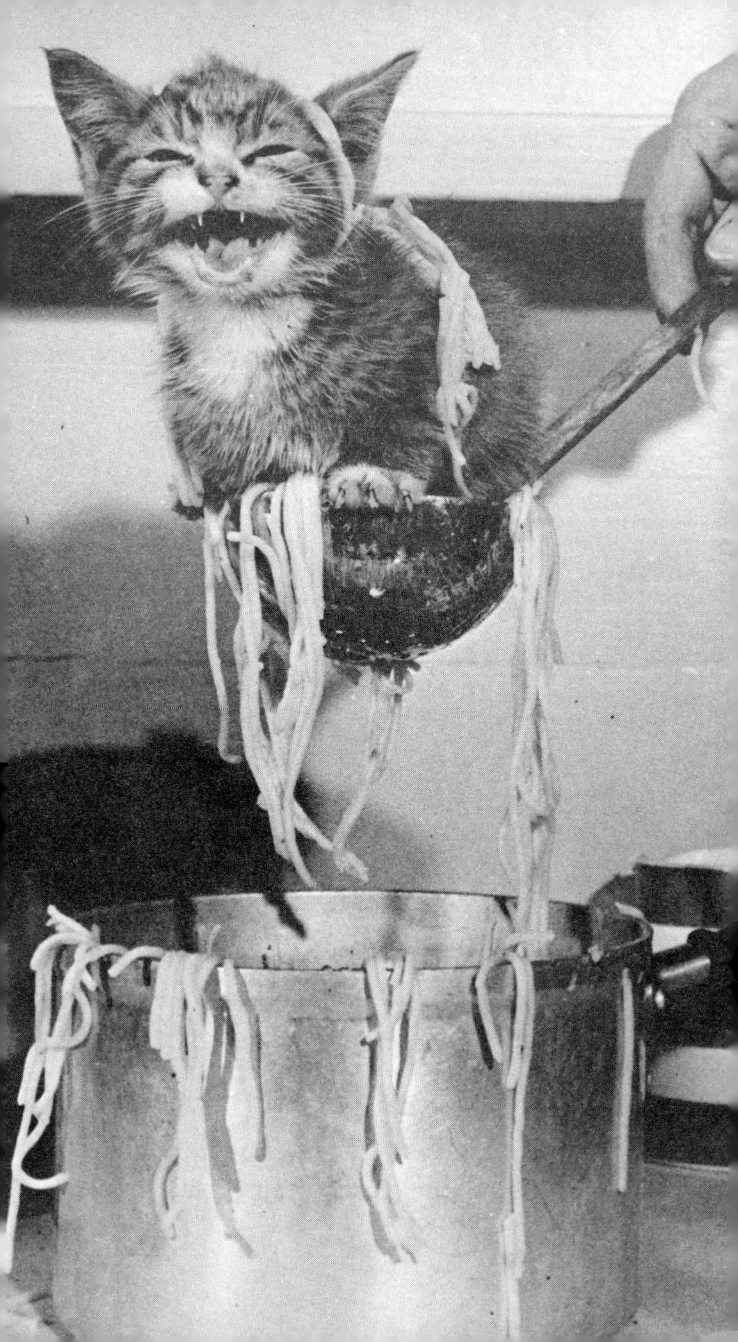

164

Exercise 63:

Is this picture funny because of unexpected presence, or absence? Both, in a way, if you stop to think about it. What in the world is a bride doing in a gambling casino? And where...oh, where...is her bridegroom? Write a short, *funny* story about the events leading up to this scene. Use your imagination, and make the plot as "far out" as you like. Make the reader laugh.

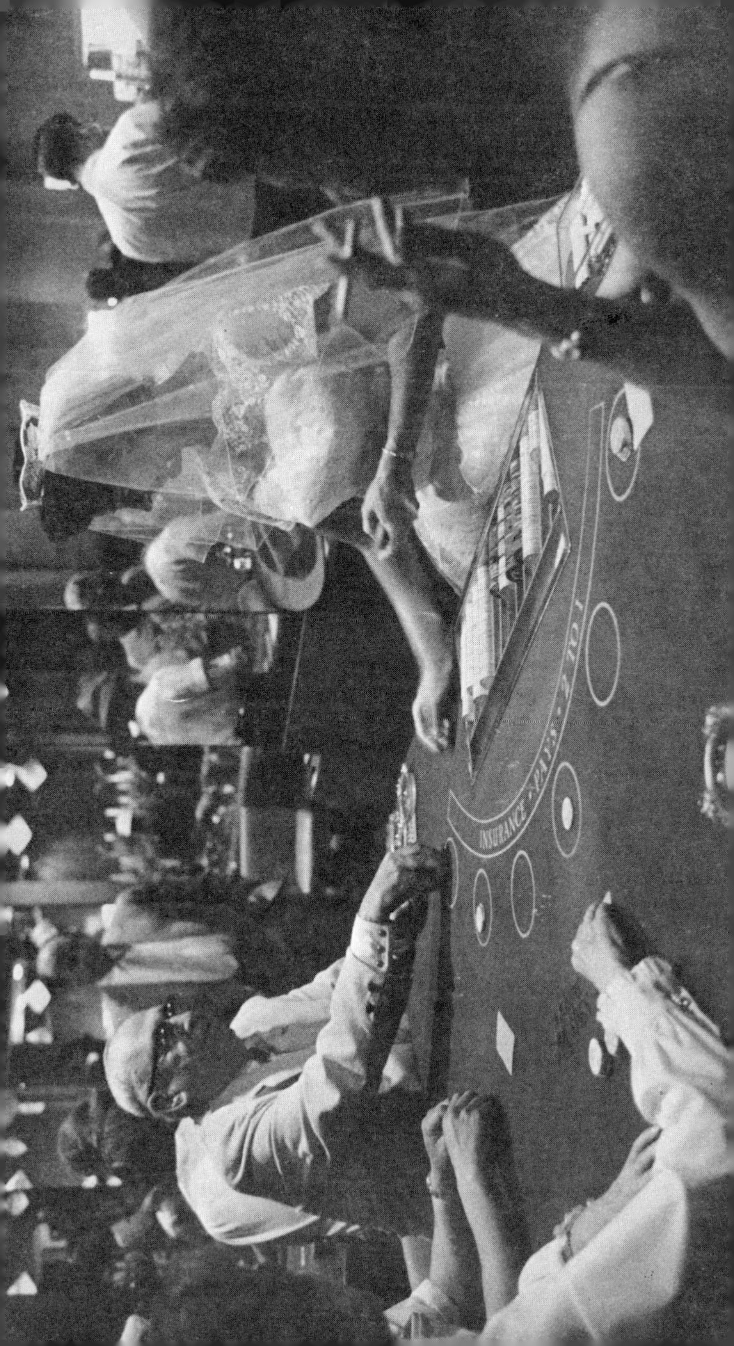
INSURANCE PAYS 2 TO 1

Funny situations often occur when the central figure is oblivious to something that other observers have seen. This is the essence of the humor in this picture. The observer sees that the boy on the billboard seems to be looking straight at the old lady, who is trudging along without realizing the picture she is causing. Her sober, old-fashioned and preoccupied appearance also makes a funny contrast to the artificially cheery, alert grins on the faces of the family.

Exercise 64:

Write a funny short story, or a long joke, about somebody very absent-minded. If you can't think of such a story or joke, describe the picture on the preceding page, making it as funny as possible. Be careful not to make the old lady a pitiful spectacle, or you will make your description sad, not funny.

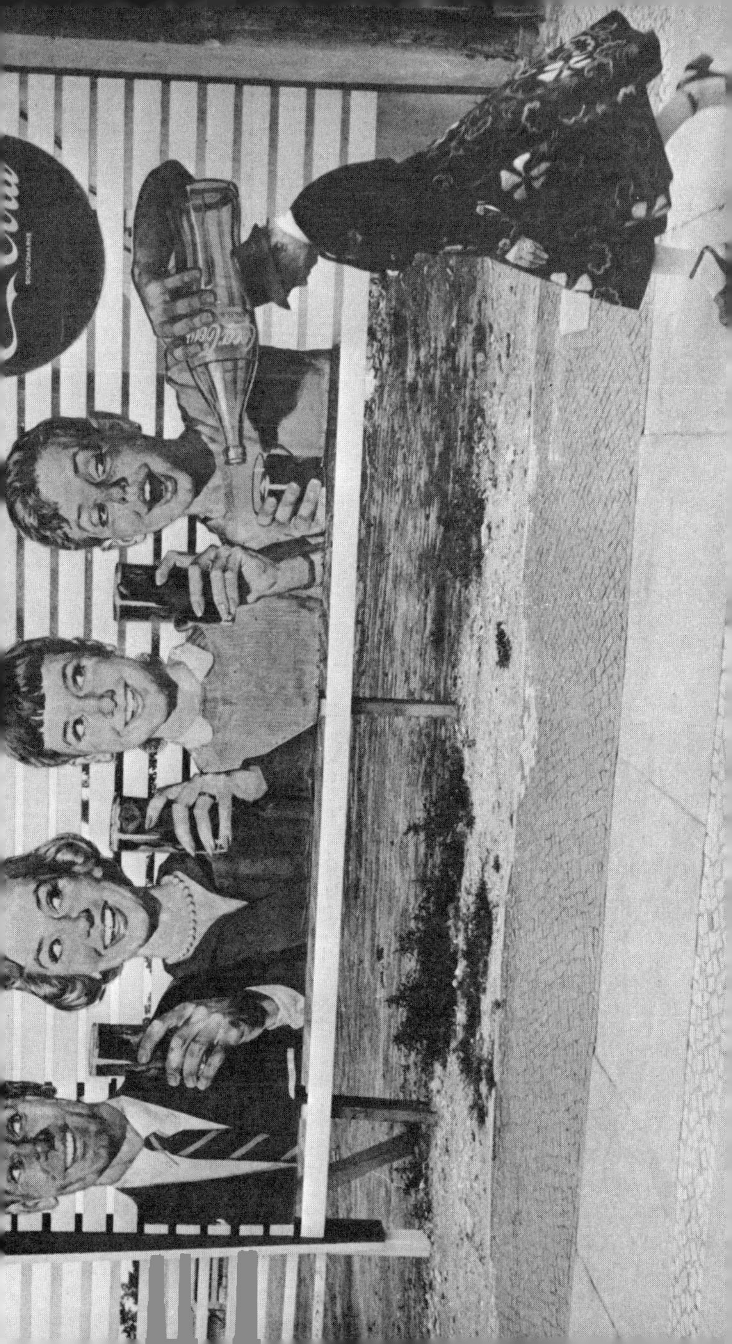

Contrast between what you'd normally expect people to do, and what they actually do, is often funny. Absent-minded people often appear funny because they do not behave as you would expect. The humor lies in the *contrast*.

Exercise 65:

What is the contrast that makes this picture funny? Are people behaving as you would expect? Write an account of the scene. Describe both the fire and the game, simultaneously, cutting from one to the other in short paragraphs. Tell the reader about the progress of both events, making the contrast between them as funny as possible.

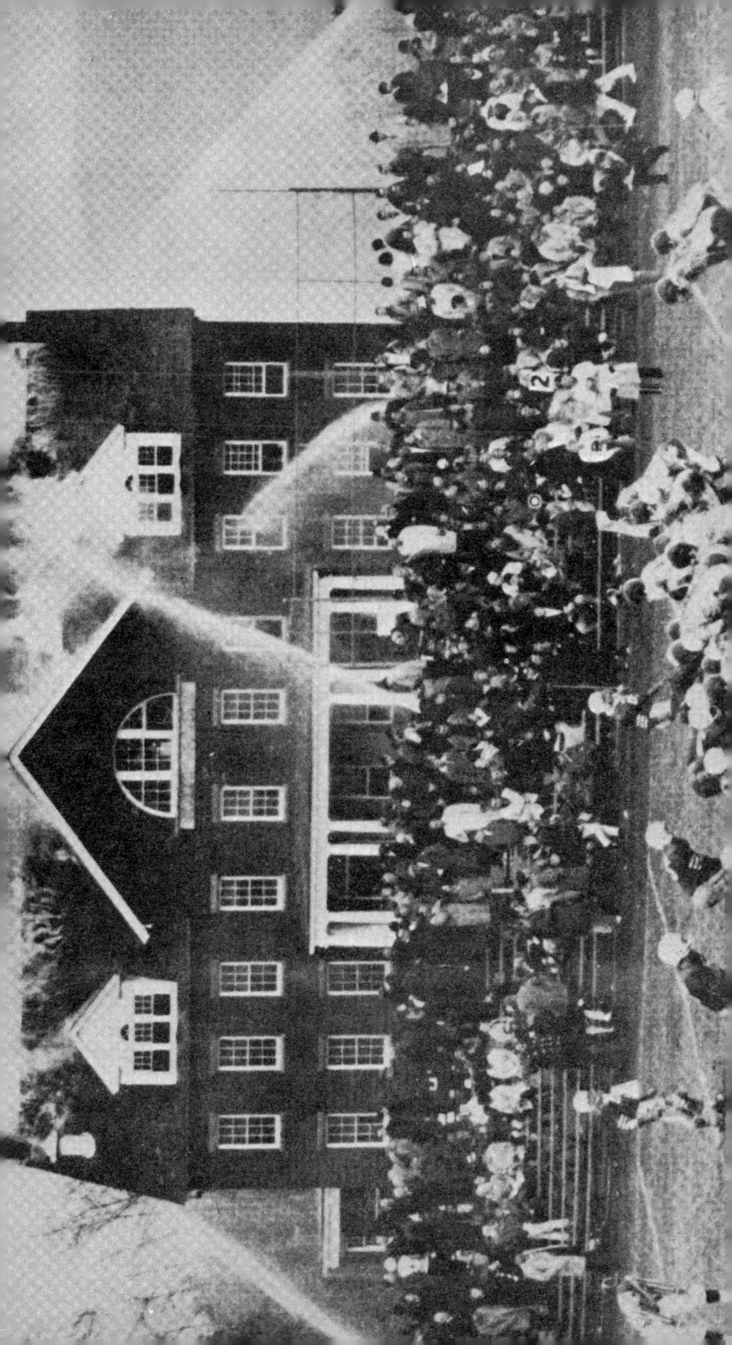

Exercise 66:

Why are children so often funny in adult eyes? Why are the women laughing at the little boy? Write a funny description of the incident, explaining the women's amusement, and making the reader laugh, too. If you prefer, write an anecdote about something very funny done by a child you know.

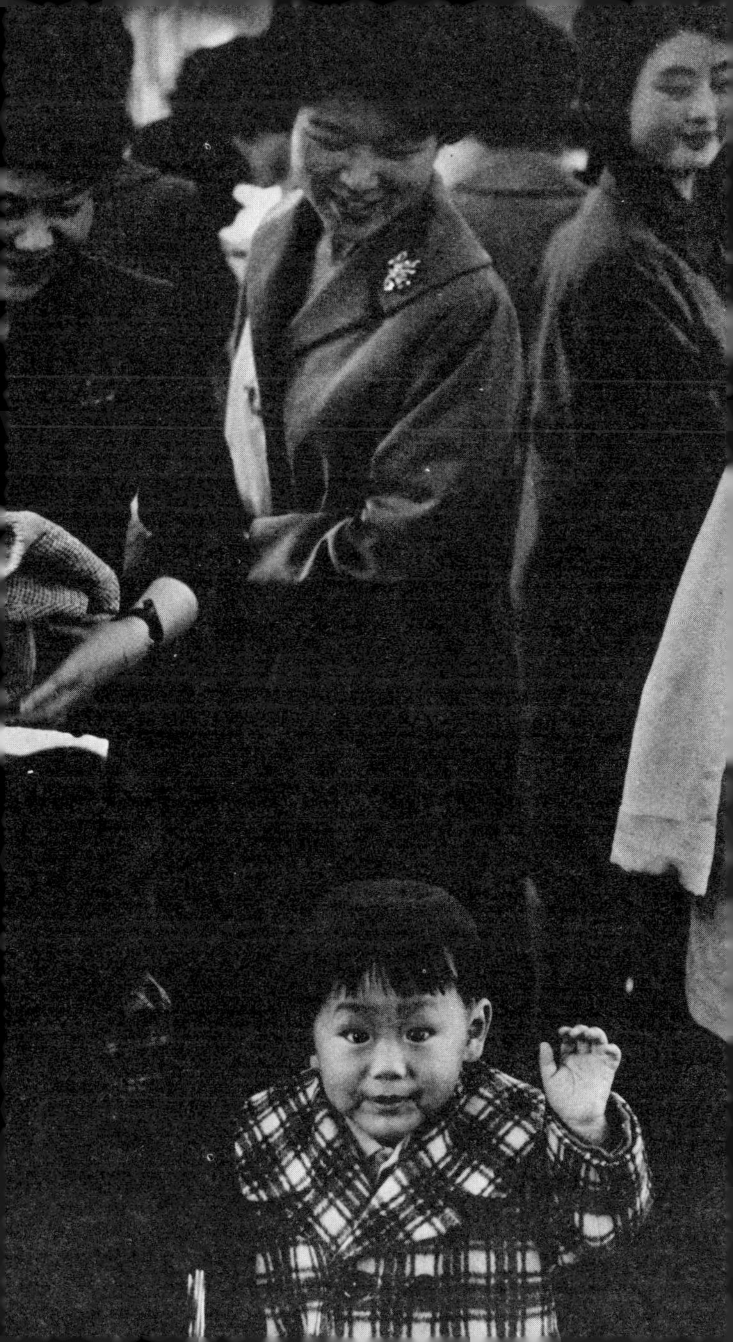

Exercise 67:

The Peruvian child is funny because her attitude is such a contrast to the two women—who are serious, totally absorbed, impassive. Describe this scene in a funny way, describing the reason for the child's expression. If you prefer, write an account of something that a child found very funny, while the adults around him didn't see the joke at all.

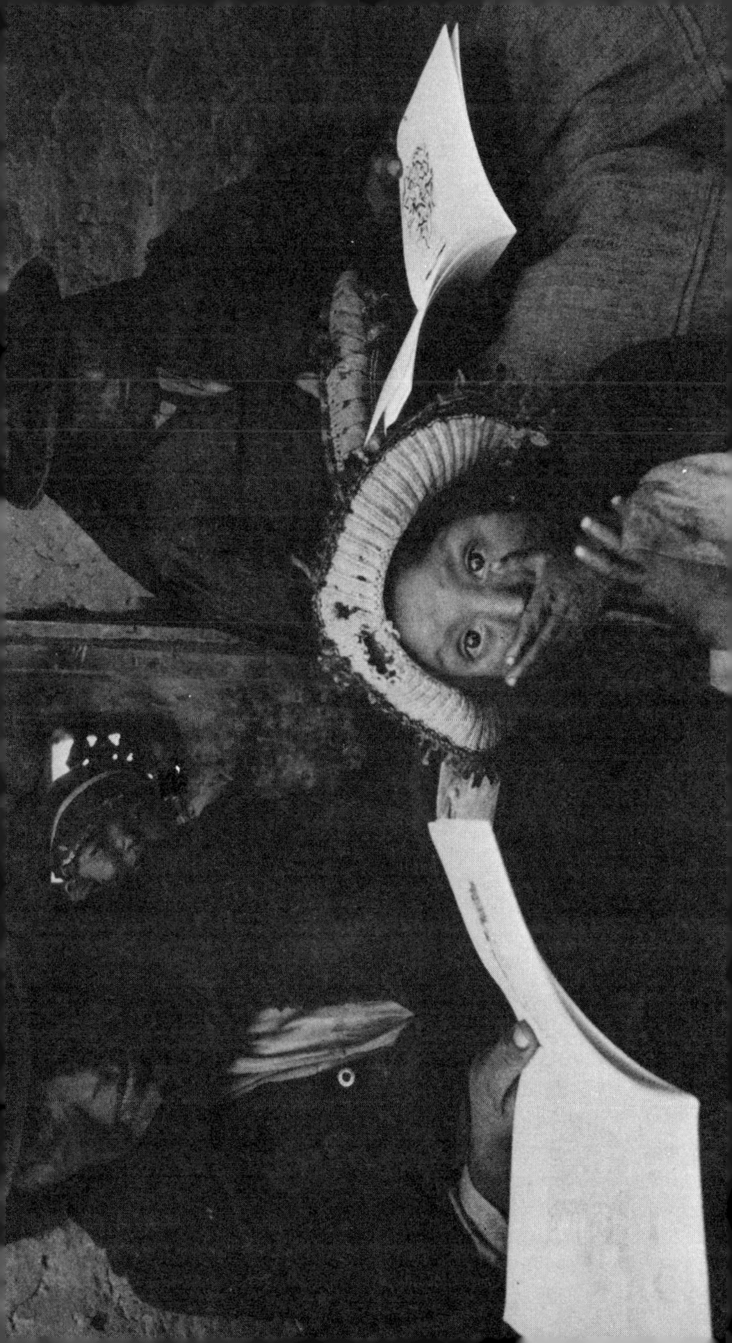

Fantasy
And
Symbolism

In a sense, all fiction is fantasy—a daydream, a vision or hallucination. Fiction may be based on a lot of observed facts, but it is not "real" in the sense that a newspaper story is real. Although he may have revealed some truth about real life, the fiction writer has created a world that exists only in his imagination.

Some of today's best writing describes worlds that are little like our own. Examples are the science-fiction stories of Arthur C. Clarke and Ray Bradbury, tales that are—literally—"fantastic."

Fantasies can be created about the future, about the distant past, and about dream worlds that never existed. The important thing is that the writer keeps his fantasy world consistent, with a certain mood and certain "laws" according to which his creatures behave.

Some writers lead their readers cleverly from the apparently real world into fantasy. Shirley Jackson's story, "The Lottery", begins with an apparently normal American country village, and ends with a nightmare-like primitive sacrifice of one of its inhabitants. Franz Kafka's "Metamorphosis" shows us a young man turning into a horrible insect, before the eyes of his horrified family.

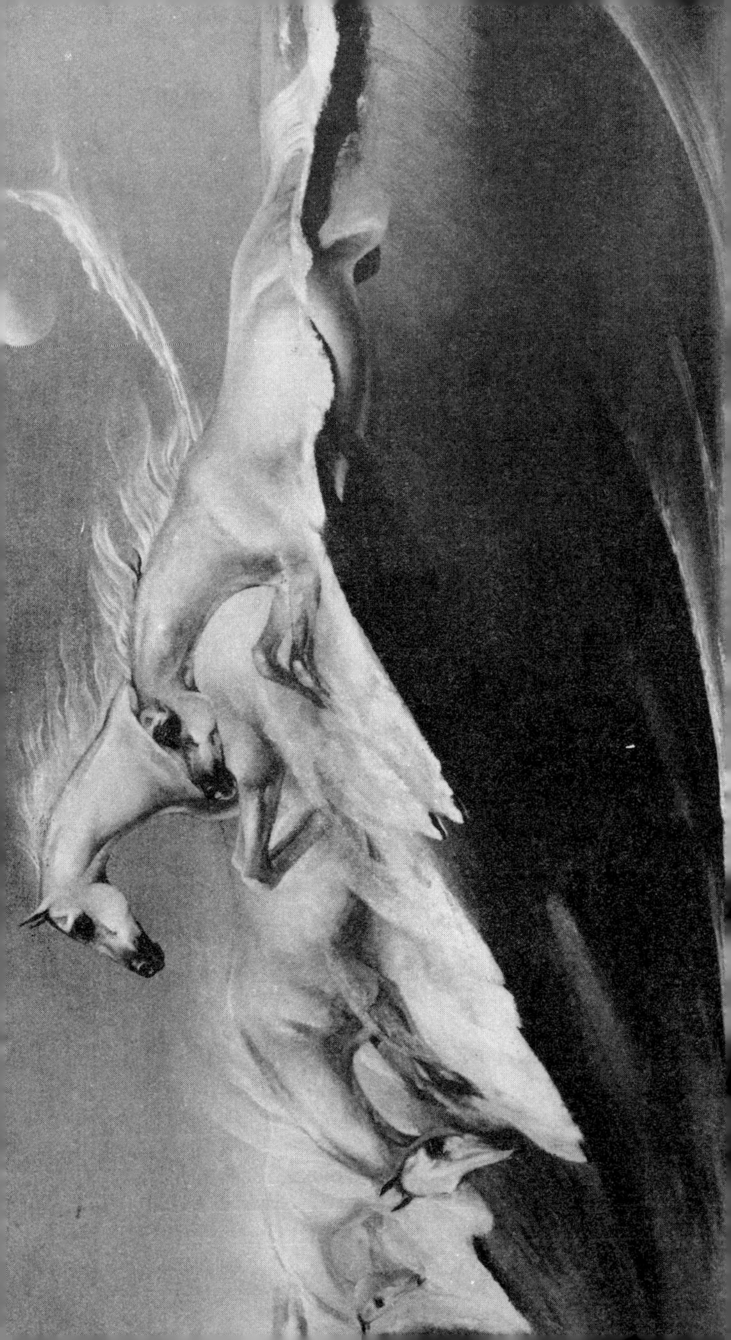

Exercise 68:

Look at this painting. Write a fantasy about it, using as much imagination as you like. Start with the real world first, then make the white caps on the waves gradually turn into the horses you see. Where do they go? Write at least half a page.

Note the way Emily Dickinson achieves a fantasy dream quality in this poem.

BECAUSE I COULD NOT STOP FOR DEATH
    Because I could not stop for Death,
    He kindly stopped for me;
    The carriage held but just ourselves
    And Immortality.

    We slowly drove, he knew no haste,
    And I had put away
    My labor, and my leisure too,
    For his civility.

    We passed the school where children played
    At wrestling in a ring;
    We passed the fields of gazing grain,
    We passed the setting sun.

    We paused before a house that seemed
    A swelling of the ground;
    The roof was scarcely visible,
    The cornice but a mound.

    Since then 'tis centuries; but each
    Feels shorter than the day
    I first surmised the horses' heads
    Were toward eternity.

Dreams are fantasies. Many of them are beautiful, seem very real, and feel to the dreamer as if they have some important "meaning."

Exercise 69:

Look at the woman with her head in her hands, and the man staring out to sea. To the left, a ship's smoke can be seen on the horizon—is it coming or going? Notice all the details in the picture—the seashells, the lighthouse, the strange fruit and driftwood, and the invisible statue on the column. Make up a "dream" story about the couple and all these objects. Give your fantasy a definite mood, and a dream-like quality. Let your imagination go. Use sensory details. Write at least two pages.

179

180

Exercise 70:

This painting is called "Americana." Look carefully at all the objects in the painting, and use them to weave another dream-like fantasy around the figure of the man. He looks relaxed. The sun is shining in this picture. The dream might be a happy one—or a nightmare. Let yourself go. Write two pages or more.

181

Many of the objects in fantasies, in our own dreams, and even in ordinary fiction, are *symbols*. They are signs or tokens, representing something else. Frequently, the thing they represent is abstract and invisible. Symbols surround us in everyday life. What does a flag stand for? What does a soldier's salute symbolize?

In fiction, always look for a deeper, hidden meaning, when an author spends a long time describing an object. The ruined, ugly and half-empty house described at the beginning of "The Fall of the House of Usher" (turn back to page 53) is a symbol. It represents the moral decay of the Usher family, and makes their disintegration visible for the reader.

A road can be the symbol of a long journey, perhaps a person's journey through life. The blue sky may, in some writing, be the symbol of infinity, happiness, purity or the unattainable. The sun stands for warmth, power, perhaps God. Rain, of course, is used in countless stories as the symbol of sadness.

Exercise 71:

Look at the soaring gull. Try to sense the "mood" of the picture. Then write down a list of all the spiritual feelings and qualities for which the bird might be a symbol.

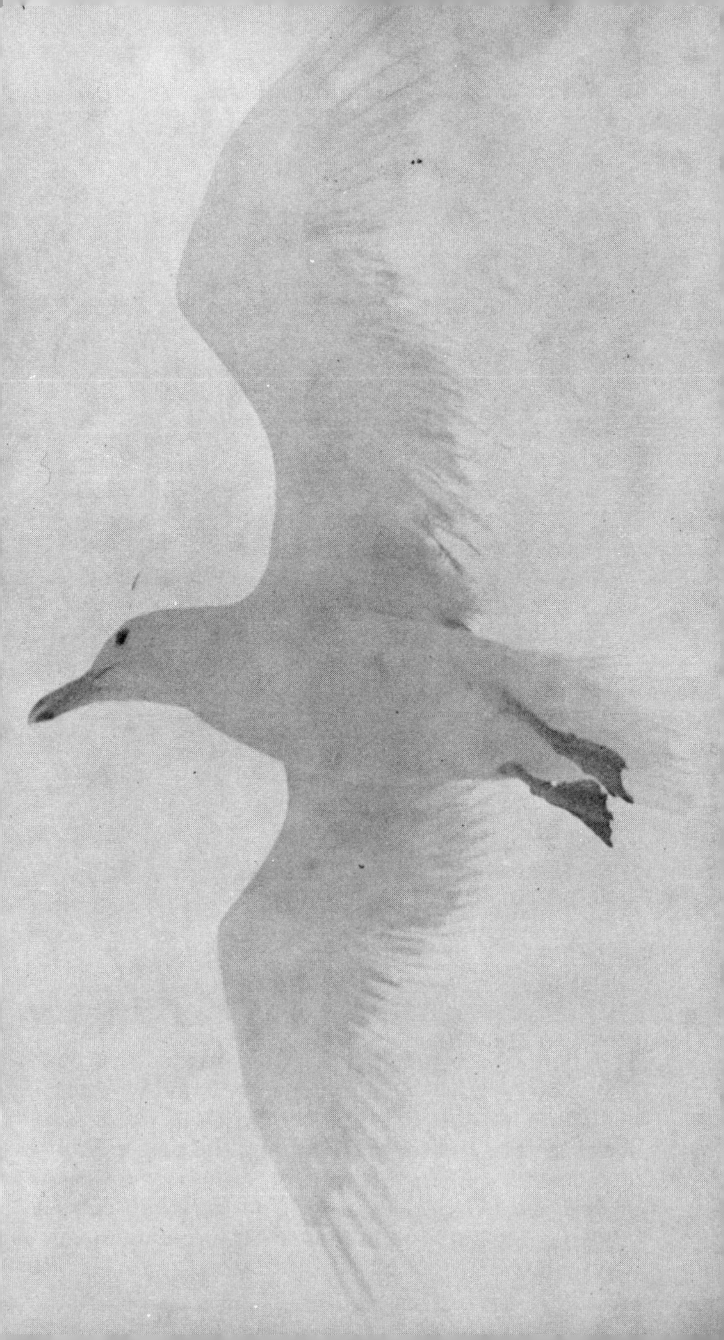

Exercise 72:

The shell is beautiful, and probably fragile. It is something precious that the girl may have found by chance, as the sea washed it up on the beach. Write a story about the girl and the shell, making the shell a symbol of something intangible in her life. If the shell is broken, what does that mean? You can write either a regular short story, set in the "real" world, or a dreamlike fantasy.

185

When an entire story is told in terms of symbols, the story is an *allegory*. Although the story seems to be a fantasy, it is about "real" life. Franz Kafka's "Metamorphosis," mentioned before, is a way of describing the shocking estrangement between the son and the rest of the family; they will not listen to him, when he tries to explain himself; they make him believe he is repulsive. Bunyan's book *Pilgrim's Progress* tells of the hero's travels to places like the Slough of Despond, the Valley of the Shadow of Death, and Vanity Fair; it is really an allegory of a Christian's spiritual progress toward perfection. Many animal stories are really allegories about people—all the way from Aesop's *Fables* to George Orwell's political satire *Animal Farm*.

Exercises 73-75:

Write one-page fantasies about the last three pictures. Try to make your fantasies serve as allegories about real life, if you can. Who is the juggler, the crowned clown tossing balls around so serenely on his high perch above the ground—and who is the little black dog watching him? Who are the eight men hiding behind their shared face? Is the mysterious rider an evil, Death-like figure, or does he seem patient and pure? Tell stories about all of them, and give your stories some inner significance. Let your imagination go... Write as much as you can.

187

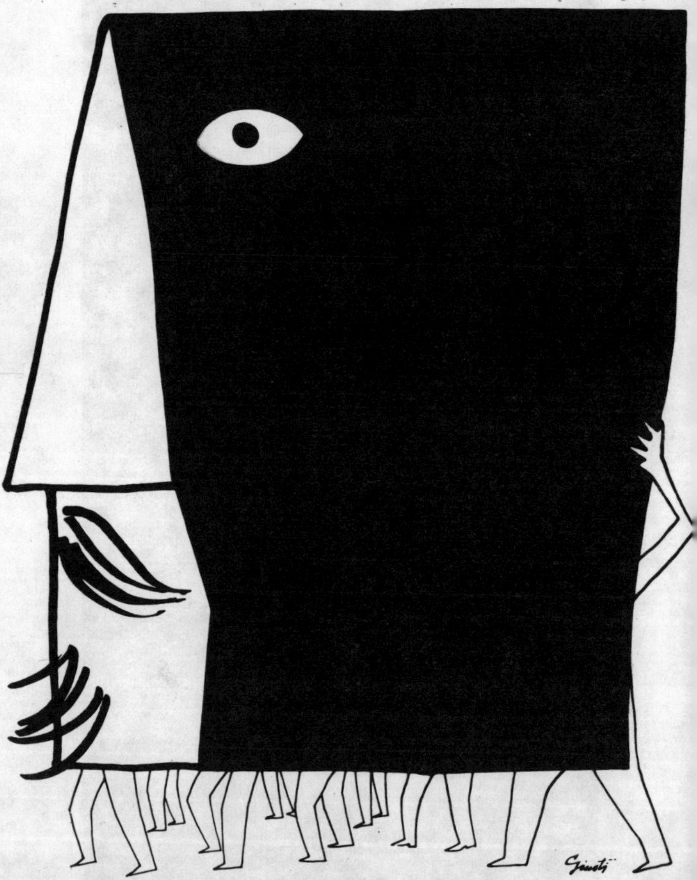

189

Acknowledgments

There are a lot of talented people in this world, and I met several of them when I did this book. To Ann Novotny of Research Reports, New York, warm thanks for her sage perspectives and excellent editorial help with this book. Also, I want to acknowledge Jean Highland's labor, kindness and editorial skill. I want to thank John Pearson, a brilliant perceptive photographer from California for his contributions to this book. He has a great eye and a fabulous future in this field. Look for his work in the magazines and elsewhere.

I am most grateful to Walt Reed and Zoltan Henczel, and the entire Famous Writers' School, Famous Artists' School staff in Westport, Connecticut for being so cooperative and enthusiastic about this project.

Much gratitude also to Scholastic Magazines, Inc. and the photography awards staff and the art awards staff. Eastman Kodak sponsors the National Student Photography Awards from which some of the photographs in this book are selected. To Jenny Copeland, to Joan

Murphy, and to Dr. William D. Boutwell, Editorial Vice President of Scholastic, I extend my sincere thanks.

Ruth Ray, an immensely talented artist, has allowed me to use photographs of her unusual paintings. I am grateful for that, and to Reid, her son, for telling me about them.

Terence Flynn also has a sharp discerning eye, and several of his photographs appear here. His work is excellent, and we should hear and see more from him later. He sings and composes music also.

My thanks also to the individual photographers, professional and amateur, who allowed me to use their pictures. Magnum, Inc. is especially deserving in this respect for their patience and understanding.

It is easy to leave out somebody important—so if I did, I apologize. People with sense do not write books, they publish them. To all the tired writers who have passed their deadlines and live in guilt-ridden despair with paralyzed fingers, I say, sooner or later, you finish.

Picture Credits

Brown Brothers—158
Famous Schools, Westport, Conn. (Zoltan Henczel, Staff Photographer)—36 Stephen Dohanos/179/181/188 Giusti
Norman Fedde—73
Terence Flynn—55/127
Rapho Guillumette—18-9 Ylla/31 E. A. Heiniger/66-7 Ron Church/75 John Bryson/94 Louis Goldman/120-1 Bob S. Smith/131 Bob S. Smith/136-7 Hanna W. Schreiber/ 154 Garry Granham/167 Lynn Millar
Ken Heyman—95/99/116/151/173
Library of Congress—97
Magnum Photos—12-3 Charles Harbutt/14 René Burri/ 16 Erich Hartmann/27 George Rodger/33 Elliott Erwitt/ 48-9 Werner Bischof/77 Charles Harbutt/92 Werner Bischof/103 Bruce Davidson/111 Eve Arnold/129 Charles Harbutt/138 Wayne Miller/142 Dennis Stock/153 Charles Harbutt/165 Inga Morath/171 Burt Glinn
Museum of Modern Art—107 Lewis H. Hine
George Novotny—46/144
John Pearson—10/24/38/40/45/50/85/88/101/ 109/112-3/114-5/125/133/161/183
Photo Researchers Inc.—71 Mathias T. Oppersdorff/ 146-7 Carl Frank
Psychology Today—57
Ruth Ray—176 photo by Walter Russell/185 photo by Walter Russell/187 photo by Peter A. Juley & Son/ 189 photo by Walter Russell
Rex Features, Ltd.—163
Scholastic Art Awards—81 water color by Mario Castillo
Scholastic Photography Awards conducted by Scholastic Magazines and Eastman Kodak Company—11 Shelby Wilson/ 15 Mark Berkley/17 Ronald Berger/60-1 Russell Handa/ 79 Glenn Moir/90 Allen Rosen
United Press International—69/169
Wide World Photos—117/149

A BANTAM PATHFINDER EDITION

STOP, LOOK & WRITE

Here is a proven way to effective writing. Based on the principle that good writing depends on accurate and keen observation, this book teaches the student to see life through the perceptive eye of the photographer and the writer. Using as examples the writing of William Faulkner, Somerset Maugham, James Joyce, Colette, Eudora Welty, Isak Dinesen and others, the student is exposed to the best of modern writing and photography.

There are chapters on using your senses, setting the scene and mood, people, point of view, conversation, dramatic tension, surprise and comedy, fantasy and symbolism and more.

PICTURES FOR WRITING
A VISUAL APPROACH TO COMPOSITION
BY DAVID A. SOHN

BANTAM PATHFINDER EDITIONS

Bantam Pathfinder Editions provide the best in
fiction and nonfiction in a wide variety of
subject areas. They include novels by classic
and contemporary writers; vivid, accurate
histories and biographies; authoritative works
in the sciences; collections of short
stories, plays and poetry.

Bantam Pathfinder Editions are carefully
selected and approved. They are durably bound,
printed on specially selected high-quality paper,
and presented in a new and handsome format.